Walking the Isle of Arran

Clan Walk Guides

Walking the Isle of Arran

Walking Scotland Series

Volume 1

Mary Welsh
and
Christine Isherwood

First published as *Forty-four Walks on the Isle of Arran*
by Westmorland Gazette, 1989
Clan Books edition, with minor revisions, published 1999
Reprinted 2003
This new and re-titled edition published Clan Books 2008

ISBN 978 1 873597 30 9

Clan Books
Clandon House
The Cross, Doune
Perthshire
FK16 6BE

Typeset by Rowland Phototypesetting Ltd,
Bury St Edmunds, Suffolk
Printed and bound in Great Britain by
St Edmundsbury Press Ltd, Bury St Edmunds, Suffolk

Publisher's Note

The Isle of Arran was the inspiration for Mary Welsh's first guide book aimed at the "average walker". This mythical creature has developed a more sophisticated and ambitious profile during the nineteen years since the publication of "Forty-four Walks on the Isle of Arran". Now Mary has returned, accompanied by co-author and artist Christine Isherwood, to re-visit fondly recalled scenes and to seek out new adventures in this haven of delight for all who relish the sensation of boots on paths and tracks, and the unique ozone- and pine-scented aroma of Scottish islands.

With WALKING THE ISLE OF ARRAN, the authors have succeeded gloriously in assembling a collection of expeditions which retains much of the flavour of the original book, but also raised its sights to satisfy the expectations of to-day's resourceful and energetic walkers. In this they have been helped enormously by the work of the Arran Access Trust, who have made great strides with opening and signposting new routes. So too the Forestry Commission, who now seem to realize the public-image advantages of encouraging walkers' access, whilst also embracing a more enlightened policy of cutting down many of their dark coniferous jungles and planting instead a balanced mix of species, including native deciduous trees.

Experienced hill-walkers will know that mountain country can be unforgiving and dangerous for the foolhardy. Newcomers to Arran and its hills should heed the authors' "Golden Rules" (see next page).

A word of praise is also due to Arran's bus services. Many Arran visitors don't take a car to the island, and it is good to know that the starting points of almost all the walks in this book can be reached from (or not very far from) a bus service. It is useful for motorists to know that they can leave their car at the start of a linear walk, and get back to it by bus from the other end.

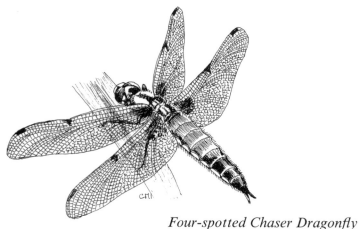

Four-spotted Chaser Dragonfly

The Authors' Golden Rules
for Good, Safe Walking

- Wear suitable clothes and take adequate waterproofs.

- Walk in strong footwear; walking boots are advisable.

- Carry the relevant map and a compass and know how to use them.

- Carry a whistle; remember six long blasts repeated at one minute intervals is the distress signal.

- Do not walk alone, and tell someone where you are going.

- If mist descends, return.

- Keep all dogs under strict control. Observe all "No Dogs" notices – they are there for very good reasons.

In all volumes of the WALKING SCOTLAND series, the authors make every effort to ensure accuracy, but changes can occur after publication. Reports of such changes are welcomed by the publisher. Neither the publisher nor the authors can accept responsibility for errors, omissions or any loss or injury.

Acknowledgements

The authors record their gratitude to Jimmy and Sandra Cochrane and Jennifer Outhwaite for their practical help during the research work for this edition.

Lamlash and the mountains from Holy Isle

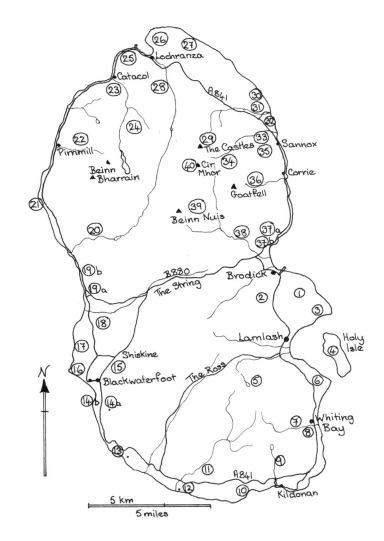

Location Map

Contents

Contents continued page 8

8

1

Dun Fionn, Clauchland Hills

Park on the west side of the A841 at grid ref 018334, the Cnoc na Dail car park. This lies opposite to a green footpath sign and a wide forest track. To access this take the A841 from Brodick and drive south for just under two miles; the car park, the second of two very close together, lies on the right side of the road.

Dun Fionn is the site of an **Iron Age fort**, dating to around 2,000 years ago, though there are no remnants to be seen now. It stands on the edge of the headland at the eastern end of the Clauchland Hills and the summit trig point is reached by a steep-ish, undulating path. Sheer cliffs defend it on one side and the land slopes sharply downwards on all other sides. The flat top is long and narrow and is covered with very short springy turf. From here the mountains to the north stand out startlingly clear. Islands float on a glassy sea; the ferry, toy-like, comes into harbour. Brodick Castle stands proud against its conifers and sheltering hills. Dun Fionn

Holy Isle from Clauchland Hills

Walk 1

provides a wonderful viewing platform for modern day walkers as it must have done for its defenders long ago.

1 Cross the road from the parking area and continue up the wide newly constructed (at the time of writing) forest road. Ignore the left turn and carry on a short way to take the easy-to-miss re-inforced slope, up the banking on the left to an open grassy area. Follow the on-going path through scattered outcrops, with some bracken and great banks of heather. Plantations stand on either side, but these lie well back from this pleasing open area. Continue up the undulating path that soon continues along a small ridge with heather on both sides. Stroll on to the cairn, where you will want to pause and enjoy this quiet place, where no traffic sounds, machinery noise or human talk intrude on its peace.

2 Go on with the path as it begins to descend, with occasional views of Holy Island to your right. Weave around rocky knolls where you might see a wheatear, and then walk on to where the open area ends and the path passes into conifers. A short way down into the trees, ignore a distinct path going off right. (This is the path you take for your return route.) As you continue to descend, look out for a short left turn that leads to the edge of a grassy platform. From here

Wheatear

you can look up the magnificent Clyde and perhaps see the ferry heading for Brodick. Go on down, quite steeply, through the trees of the forest to pass through a gate. Then cross a track, and climb the stile ahead.

3 Beyond, wind a little left and then climb uphill. After a short descent into a hollow, climb steeply to the trig point. Take a long break here to enjoy the superb views. Then return to climb the stile and retrace your route up through the conifers to reach the left turn (a cyclists' route), ignored earlier. Here you need to make a decision. You may wish to return by your outward route or you might like to be a little more adventurous. The path, very good to start with, continues for all its way through the forest. It is wet in places after heavy rain, and is sometimes flooded. It is also very sheltered if the weather has deteriorated.

4 As you progress along the forest path and come to a flooded area, look for the cyclists' waymarks pinned to trees, on the right, that direct you along a lengthy diversion into the forest, keeping parallel with the path, to circumvent the water. Eventually you arrive at a large area of clear-fell and, again at the time of writing, the path deteriorates. This path leads you to join, with a scramble, the new forest road. A short way down the latter, look for a grassy left turn (unsigned), follow this path to reach the Dunan Mor Cairn. In this Bronze Age burial mound a jet necklace was found. Now only two stones stand upright and two lie lengthwise on either side. Behind the cairn is a small hillock, covered with heathers, bilberry, tiny rowans and a mass of flowering grasses.

Bilberry

11

5 Return a few steps along the grassy path and turn left along another. This runs parallel with the forest road and eventually joins it. Continue on to the car park.

Birch catkins

Practicals

Type of walk: In the past this was always a most enjoyable walk. Today the forest road has cut through parts of the footpaths but, as the road is not complete, the authors are sure that the FC will reinstate them with signposts etc. Even so it remains a must for walkers especially when the heather is in flower.

Total distance:	5 miles/8km
Time:	3 hours
Maps:	OS Explorer 361/Landranger 69

2

Glen Cloy

Park in the Cnoc na Dail car park, grid ref 018334, as for walk 1.

This walk makes use of excellent paths put in by the **Arran Access Trust** (AAT). The aims of the trust are to improve access, restore and repair paths and to reconcile differences over access and provision. The trust has also improved signing, added interpretation panels and produced leaflets to help with the understanding of Arran's natural heritage.

At the end of this walk you may wish to visit a **group of standing stones**. Four large stones stand upright with several small stones between surrounded by a sea of sweet smelling heather. The circle probably dates from the Bronze Age. Its purpose may

Fairy Glen, Brodick

never be fully ascertained – maybe they were used as a crude calendar in conjunction with the stars or perhaps they were burial sites or scenes of ancient rituals. From the circle there is a superb view of Beinn Nuis, Beinn a'Chliabhain and Goatfell.

1 From the small car park, take the forest road (main track) out of the top left corner. Walk up the slope and take the first right turn to continue on another wide road through the forest from where you have a wonderful view of the northern mountains ahead of you. Carry on through a large area of clear-fell. Then as the track swings left a little you can see into Glen Cloy, with Muileann Gaoithe and Torr Maol towering over the valley.

Walk 2

2 Follow the track as it carries on down and down, with conifers to the right and earlier clear-fell to the left. Here heather, rush and a few deciduous trees line the way, hiding the serried ranks of conifers beyond. Go on descending now with, immediately ahead, the fine amphitheatre of hills with white-topped waterfalls slashing the slopes. Cross the Gleann Dubh burn by a bridge, then follow the way as it begins to climb for a short distance and then becomes a fine reinforced narrow path.

3 Carry on along the path through conifers where the verges are bright with heather and cushions of moss. Soon the path continues along a little ridge, high above Glencloy Water on the right and a small tributary to the other side, racing to join the main river. Then cross the tributary by a footbridge and walk on to a kissing gate. Head on along a good path across a rushy meadow to pass under a row of beeches. Go on over the next meadow to come close to the Glencloy Water once more. Look left for a fine view of Goatfell and then pass through a gate to walk a track,

14

still with the river below you, to the right. To your left tranquil pastures stretch away, sloping up to the foot of the hills and here you might spot a long-legged hare.

4 Where the track swings away left to two white-painted dwellings, stroll on ahead on the signposted footpath, 'Brodick 1 mile'. Stride on towards the Auchrannie Hotel and then follow the continuing way with the river still to your right and holiday chalets to the left, soon to join the A-road. Turn right and cross the bridge over Glencloy Water and walk on along the main road until you can turn right towards Brodick's post office, which lies back on a side road. Climb the ongoing road, passing in front of the post office, for 400yds/440m. Turn right and walk up a lane signposted for Lamlash. Ignore all side turns and go on where it becomes a rising track, hedged on both sides. Then the way levels and the countryside opens out with heather, gorse and birch stretching away on the right and pastures to the left.

5 Eventually the well-reinforced way descends delightfully through scattered birch woodland and lives up to its name 'The Fairy Glen'. Carry on through a large area of clear-fell, cross a tributary stream by a footbridge and walk on beside it. Then re-cross the stream once more and climb steadily through more clear-fell on the good path, which leads you into a picnic area just beside the A841. From here take the path, signed 'Lamlash' and walk on the pleasing way to arrive at the car park from where you started the walk.

Brown hare

6 Before you leave, you might wish to make the following diversion to visit the stone circle seen across the A-road. Cross with care and take a narrow grassy path, between young birch trees, that lies to the left of the wide forest road. A short distance along, just before the plantation, turn left and walk a little path that takes you to the circle. Return by the same paths.

Crossed-leaved Heath

Bell Heather

Practicals

Type of walk: Most pleasing walk through forest and woodland, and a short diversion to a stone circle, with delightful views for much of the way. Good paths and forest tracks.

Total distance:	6 miles/9.8km plus ¼ mile/0.5km
Time:	3–4 hours
Maps:	OS Explorer 361/Landranger 69

3

Clauchlands Cliffs

Park in the well signed large parking area, on the shore side, where the Margnaheglish road turns sharp left to Clauchlands farm, grid ref 049326. To reach this, turn left off the A841 at the foot of the hill as you approach Lamlash from the direction of Brodick. Drive for 1¼ miles/2km. The car park has a convenient seat for putting on your boots.

Lamlash is one of Arran's main settlements and is situated on the east-coast, conveniently sheltered from the prevailing wind. From the cliffs you have spectacular views over Lamlash Bay, Holy Island and across the Firth to mainland Ayrshire. As you climb watch out for gannets, kittiwakes and various gulls. On this walk you also come close to one of the Forestry Commission's (FC) plantations. The FC first came to Arran in 1950 with the purchase of 670 hectares from the Fullerton family. Over the years further land was purchased and now over 7700 hectares have been planted.

1 Walk on from the parking area, go through the gate and on along a track, muddy in parts, with the sea to your right. At a low 'Coastal

Dun Fionn

Walk 3

Way' sign, ignore the continuing track and also a wide track cut for a short way into the hillside, on your left. Between the two, the arrow directs walkers, obliquely, up an indistinct grassy trod, between scattered gorse. Continue on along the edge of the grassy hill to come to a fence. Cross a stile and begin your long ascent outside an ancient wall now enclosed by two wire fences. The narrow path for much of the way is sunken and the low bank (probably an old barrier to prevent stock from falling over the cliff), to the right, is quite comforting as you climb higher and higher up the huge cliffs. Stop to enjoy the incredible views of the two Cumbrae islands, the mainland, and the wide expanse of sea where you might spot the ferry heading for Brodick.

2 The path climbs for nearly three-quarters of a mile to a fence corner. Here you may wish to climb the clear path, which moves away from the cliff edge to the trig point on Dun Fionn (see walk 1). If you wish to avoid the extra ascent, walk beside the fence, inland, over some quite rough grass, then move right to join the path coming down from the trig point and follow the way over a low mound to climb a stile to a junction of paths. Here you might wish to make a diversion by descending the path, on your right, to a seat from where there is an extensive view over the delightful flat land about the Corriegills, with Brodick and the Arran mountains beyond.

3 Return to the junction of paths and, leaving the stile on your left, descend a clear path for over a quarter of a mile, along the outside of the forest, keeping the trees to your right. Go through the kissing gate and beyond strike diagonally right across a pathless

18

Kittiwake

wet pasture to a hedge and a signpost. Then cross a stream by a small wooden bridge. Beyond, wind round left to a waymarked post and then drop downhill, very slightly right, to climb a stile to the left of a cottage. Turn right and follow the farm track past Clauchlands Cottage, where the track bears half right and climbs uphill.

4 Just before a gate across the track, take a stile, on the left, to descend a narrow path through scrub. Climb the next stile and follow the little path to a burn, which you step across to carry on down the lovely way, with the burn chuckling beside you hidden deep beneath lush vegetation, to join a metalled road at Prospect Hill. Go on downhill to join the shore road, where you turn left to walk the pleasing way to the car park.

Practicals

Type of walk: A delightful walk beside the shore before climbing dramatic cliffs to the fort or its ramparts. The return is made down beside the forest, then through pastures and along farm tracks. Take care on a very short stretch of exposed cliff. Do not attempt in a southerly gale.

Total distance:	3 miles/5km
Time:	2 hours
Maps:	OS Explorer 361/Landranger 69

4

Holy Isle

Park at Lamlash Pier, grid ref 029313. Lamlash lies on the east coast of Arran, 3½ miles/5.5km south of Brodick.

Holy Isle takes its name from its association with St Molaise. It was once known as Eilean na Molaise, the Isle of Molaise. The name Lamlash now given to the village is a corruption of Molaise. In the 6th century the saint spent several years in a cave on the island, mortifying his flesh, as was the custom, in preparation for becoming a missionary.

Pillar Rock Lighthouse, Holy Isle

The island lies off the south-east coast of Arran, opposite the delightful village of Lamlash. Its high hill, **Mullach Mor**, 1026ft/314m, gives shelter to the village and to Lamlash Bay.

The island was bought by a **Buddhist community** from a private owner and now visitors are most welcome. It is officially designated as a UK Sacred Site. It is a natural sanctuary for birds and animals and there is an indigenous tree planting programme. At the south end there is a closed Buddhist retreat and at the north end there is the Centre

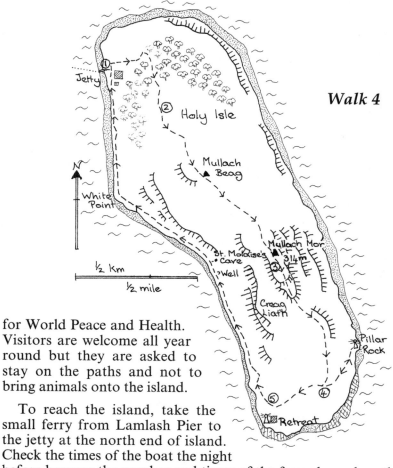

for World Peace and Health. Visitors are welcome all year round but they are asked to stay on the paths and not to bring animals onto the island.

To reach the island, take the small ferry from Lamlash Pier to the jetty at the north end of island. Check the times of the boat the night before because the number and times of the ferry depend on the tide and the weather. The crossing takes 10 minutes and visitors are met by a member of the community. The ferry does not run in the winter except by request.

1 Disembark at the jetty and walk the walled route to a plaque displaying a map of the island. Turn left and cross the grass behind the shore to an opening marked by two prayer flags and a small notice with an arrow 'To the Top'. Turn right as directed and walk up the field to a stile. Cross into a developing woodland of birch and rowan and with planted ash and oak. Wind left,

21

then right, and carry on to a stile at the top. In spring primroses and bluebells abound. Beyond the stile, follow the sign directing you up through heather. Climb steadily with occasional grassy sunny hollows favoured by the animals that live here – horses, goats and Soay sheep. The horses and Soay sheep have been introduced relatively recently but now are feral. Goats are thought to date from the time of the Vikings who put them on the island to be a readily available source of food.

2 In places the climbing is steep and the path eroded but hold on to the heather which is old and tough and assists your ascent. Do not be tempted by the animal tracks, which go off to contour round the hillside. The walkers' path keeps climbing. Usually there is a neat sign to show you the way. After another steep climb you reach the rocky summit of Mullach Beag, from where there are splendid views north to the Arran mountains and south to Ailsa Craig. Go on to descend into a small col and then up a steep path with some scree, followed by a rock scramble with good handholds. Beyond, the walking is easy and soon you reach the trig point, adorned with old prayer flags, on Mullach Mor. The views are superb.

3 Continue along the narrow ridge and then descend, gently at first, but soon more steeply down a rocky staircase where paths proliferate. Look ahead and choose your own route down. Soon you reach a gentler slope and then can follow the ridge above the east coast. You are recommended to stay on the path, which is marked with ropes, because there are deep clefts and fissures in the rocks at the side. Then go on down through the heather to join a path that crosses the island.

4 Turn left and walk 230yds/200m to see Pillar Rock lighthouse in its very dramatic setting. Return and continue along the good wide path in the direction of a second lighthouse. A small wooden cabin above it is the home of the Lama Yeshe Rimpoche, who is the chief Buddhist

Soay sheep

on the island. Go through a gap in a wall and continue towards the lighthouse but, before you reach it, turn right through a gate. This avoids disturbing people who are on retreat in the original lighthouse keepers' cottages.

5 Beyond the gate, the good path leads you back along the coast. As you go look for Buddhist rock paintings, a spring with a copper ladle so that you may sample the healing holy water and also visit St Molaise's cave. Look for Soay sheep, oyster catchers and eiders. Enjoy the fine views across Lamlash Bay to the village and the hills. When you arrive at the information centre and café enjoy the tea or coffee provided by a Buddhist before returning to the jetty for the boat.

Walk 4b

For those walkers who do not wish to climb over the hill, turn right along the shore from the jetty. The path is distinct and level and there is much to see. Look for Soay sheep and goats on the shore. Look for horses up on the hills, on the skyline and also on the shore. Look out to sea to enjoy the wealth of bird life. The path, at first, passes by a planting of indigenous trees. Then as it moves on and comes close to the crags, notice the caves, the paintings, the lush vegetation and the many wild flowers that border the path throughout spring and summer. After 1¾ miles/3km you reach a gate, where you are asked to turn left to avoid disturbing the people on retreat who live in the cottages once inhabited by the keepers of the south-west lighthouse. You may wish to carry on over a pasture or as far as Pillar Rock lighthouse, a level walk and just round the corner of the ridge, before returning by the same route.

Practicals

Type of walk: A rugged hill climb followed by a level return along the coast.

Distance:	4½ miles/7km
Time:	3 hours
Maps:	OS Explorer 361/Landranger 69

To check times of ferry crossings tel 01770 600998

5

Urie Loch

Park in Dye Mill car park, grid ref 015298. To access this take the A841 south from Brodick to pass through Lamlash, and turn right into The Ross and drive on for ½ mile/1km. The car park lies on the left side of the road in a forest clearing.

Spreading rapidly over the forest floor exposed after clear-felling is the invasive **salmon berry plant**. It has delightful pink flowers in the summer and rich red berries in the autumn. The forestry commission have had to introduce a policy of spraying the young bushes to stop them crowding out most other plants. It adds to the list of invaders that have taken over parts of our countryside, such as Himalayan balsam and Japanese knotweed.

1 From the parking area return to the main forest track, turn right to cross the bridge and go through the barrier which has several signs on it. After a few steps, turn right along a narrow path,

North Arran hills from the path to Urie Loch

signposted Urie Loch. Cross the footbridge over the burn and follow the well made track up beside the hurrying water. Pass under conifers and go up steps, with the pretty burn still to your left. Ignore the next footbridge (on the left) and follow the sign for the loch. Then go on up through the clear-fell where you should pause to enjoy the superb views of Lamlash and Holy Isle. In spring the forest floor is extensively carpeted in bluebells.

2 The path then moves into woodland, with deciduous trees on either side, and conifers stretching away beyond. It can be muddy underfoot and it is easier to walk to the right side of the wide, climbing ride. When you reach a waymarked level clearing, enjoy a little warming sun after the dense shade. Follow a shorter, steep climb where you should still keep to the right side (unless there has been a drought) and then the path reaches a wide ride with banks of heather on either side.

Walk 5

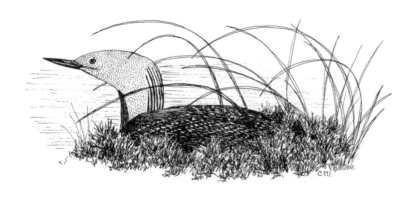

Red-throated diver

25

3 Follow the ride as it winds round as directed by a waymark. This path is grassy underfoot and leads to a large clearing. Beyond, a steep, narrow climb continues to the next waymark and on to an open area in the forest, where in spring you might hear a cuckoo. The path goes on left along the base of the steep-sided, heather clad slope of The Urie hill (1366ft/425m), and just above the top edge of the forest. From here the views of Holy Isle are good. The path then takes you up a very short steep rocky scramble and after this the forest is left behind.

4 Follow the path as it takes you out onto the moorland to pass a white post, indicating the way. Carry on the wide path, from where you might spot a hen harrier quartering the heather. Head on to the lip of a large basin in which lies the lonely mountain loch. Look down to see the man-made island, constructed to encourage red-throated divers to nest. You may wish to descend a path to the side of the loch. Beyond the pool is pathless boggy moorland, leading to a very distant trig point on Tighvein 1341ft/ 458m. Before leaving the rim, climb a short way, right, to reach a hillock, the highest point on The Urie.

Cuckoo

5 Return by the same route through the forest, enjoying the splendid view of the northern hills, until you reach the footbridge ignored early on the way up. This time cross the bridge and bear left to follow the burn through bluebell woodland. Look for waterfalls and lovely cascades on this glorious burn, a great contrast with the bleak moorland and the dark severe forest. Cross the next footbridge and go down steps to return to the parking area.

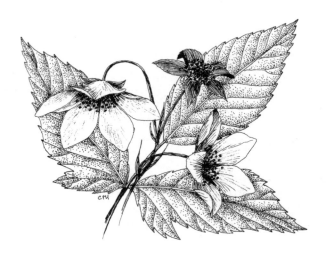

Salmonberry

Practicals

Type of walk: A challenging walk with some superb views. Tracks can be muddy. Both paths along the side of the burn are delightful. The loch is set in a quiet lonely hollow and is well worth the effort required to reach it.

Total distance:	5 miles/8km
Time:	3 hours
Maps:	OS Explorer 361/Landranger 69

6

Kingscross

Park at the Dyemill car park, grid ref 015298, as for walk 5.

The car park is named after an **old water-driven mill** that stood here and was involved with the finishing process of woven cloth. **The Ross** is one of two inland roads that cross the island from coast to coast. The road runs from Lamlash, through Glen Scorrodale and then reaches the west coast, and the A841 once again, south of Sliddery.

King's Cross Dun dates from around late BC to early AD. It has a fine outer rampart and standing on this you can appreciate its wise choice of site for a fort. Also on this promontory, to the landward side of the fort, is a **boat-shaped burial ground**, where it is believed a Viking, and his boat, was interred around the 9th century AD.

Kingscross and Holy Isle

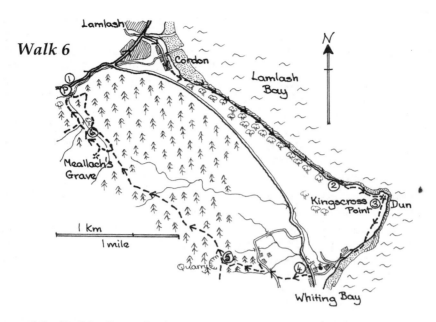

Walk 6

Meallach's Grave is the site of a Neolithic (about 6,000 years ago) chambered tomb believed to have been in use for 1,000 years. It has two entrance stones and at its head a large slab of stone. Lower down the hillside is the site of Lagaville village, which was occupied until the late 19th century when it was finally abandoned and the occupants rehoused in Lamlash.

1 Leave the car park, right, to descend The Ross, with the Monamore Burn, tumbling down to your right. At the A-road, cross and walk left for ¼ mile/0.5km then turn right along the signposted lane for Cordon. Stroll the quiet way to the end of the road and go on where it becomes a track. Then take a grassy trod on to the beach to walk right, with Lamlash Bay and lovely Holy Island to your left. The shore is pebbly and after a storm much slippery seaweed is washed up. There are faint traces of a path but at times you have to step from one grassy tuft to the next one, with rivulets of sea water between. Carry on along the shore, now with a fish farm between you and Holy Isle. Pause as you go to look for seals, mergansers, eiders and redshanks. Eventually, after 1¾ miles/3km of quite hard walking you arrive at the pontoon jetty for the fish farm.

2 Climb up onto to it, cross it, and then join a continuing good track. When you can see a house, through the trees to your right, go on along a grassy path, running parallel with the shore. Remain on the grassy trod, which is pleasingly soft on your feet after the beach. Keep well above a bouldery stretch to descend a little to reach a well-placed seat. Then stroll on, gently climbing, always remaining on the grassy way, nearest to the shore. Look ahead to see the prominent pointed cairn on a hillock above Kingscross Point and carry on towards it to reach the Iron Age fort, a fascinating mound with a small rampart surrounding it. Then perhaps seek out the site of the Viking burial.

3 Walk on ahead, keeping parallel with the sea, passing through large stretches of well tended grass, bordered with bracken and scattered trees. Climb steadily along a narrower grassy trod, still in sight of the sea. When you can see the houses on the outskirts of Whiting Bay, bear left on a path through bushes on the edge of now shallower cliffs. Ignore the track down to the shore (this has a cable across it preventing access). Cross a stile and go along the edge of a field to pass through a kissing gate and carry on, soon to descend a narrow track. After the next stile the narrow grassy path descends between gorse and bracken to another stile and then the beach. Beyond, walk on along the shore, soon to join a wide track, with the sea still to your left and scattered houses to your right. On reaching a narrow road, turn left, cross a bridge and go on along the way to come to a car park, on the shore side, and opposite the striking sandstone Whiting Bay and Kildonan Church, with its tall bell tower. Walk on to come to the side of the A841, which you cross and bear left.

4 A few yards/metres along, take the signposted road on your right, which climbs quite steeply. Keep straight ahead on a track, when the road turns right to a dwelling. Go on uphill along this

Merganser

30

pleasing way, which can be muddy after heavy rain. Look for great sheets of liverworts on the right bank and, on the left, huge cushions of moss. At the end of the track, turn right onto a narrow road and stroll on, the way soon shadowed by conifers. As you go, look for the signed access track into the trees, on the left, and follow it left on its undulating way. At first it passes through the dark plantation and then you pass through a wall into a lighter section of pines to come to the edge of a sandstone quarry.

5 Turn right onto a cycle way and follow it as it arcs a little way round the edge of the quarry, on your left. Stride on the right of two ongoing tracks, following the waymarks, to descend into more of the forest before climbing again through a large area of clear-fell, with a fine view over to Holy Isle and glimpses of the northern mountains. Watch out for the marker post directing you left into the trees, signed Meallach's Grave. Follow the narrow path as it carries on beside the trees on your right, with more clear-fell to your left, to reach a sign directing you uphill into the clear-fell to see the grave. Then return to the path beside the trees and go on down. Look for a signboard for the village of Lagaville, with no obvious trace of the settlement to be seen. Go downhill and wind right round a pool.

6 At a junction of paths, ignore the acute right turn that leads to a bridge. Instead carry on to cross the bridge ahead. Follow the

Grey wagtail

31

path as it winds right, to descend with a cascading burn to your right. Go on downhill to cross two more bridges and on to arrive at the Dyemill car park.

Heron

Practicals

*Type of walk: The beach makes for quite hard walking but from it there are delightful views. This part should be attempted at **low tide** because at Spring tides, the sea covers the shore and for quite a long way there is no chance of retreating into the forest or up the high cliffs. (Tide tables obtained from the TIC).*

Total distance:	7½ miles/12km
Time:	4 hours
Maps:	OS Explorer 361/Landranger 69

7

Glenashdale Falls

Park at Whiting Bay, grid ref 048253. The large parking area lies beside the bus shelter on the sea side of the A841, at the south side of the Glenashdale Burn and the south end of the village.

Glenashdale Falls

The southern end of Arran is made up of massive horizontal sills of hard igneous rock alternating with layers of softer rocks. Over time, streams have worn down and cut through the softer rocks but they have had very little effect on the harder rocks, resulting in several spectacular waterfalls. At **Glenashdale** the upper falls drop 40ft/ 12m and the lower falls plunge a further 90ft/28m.

The **new viewing platform** is constructed of robust timber, which appears to 'take off' into the air above the trees and rocks below, supported by steel girders

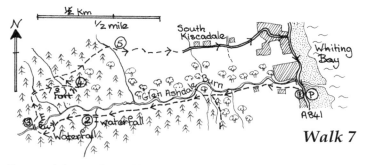

Walk 7

cantilevered from the solid rock. From this magnificent vantage point the whole trajectory of the falls can be seen at once. The waterfalls are impressive in dry conditions but after a long spell of rain they are awesome.

1 Cross the road from the parking area to take a metalled road, signposted 'Glenashdale Falls'. Stroll on where the road becomes a track and follow the glorious way with, to your right, the burn racing towards the sea. Go through a gate into the forest. Walk on the rising way through deciduous woodland and continue on the excellent path. Ignore the signed left turn for the 'Giants' Grave' (see walk 8). Go on to cross a tributary stream on bright red sandstone slabs and then after half a mile the path begins to climb through trees along the side of the gorge. Ahead, another white-topped feeder stream crosses the path, tumbling down the steep slopes to reach the Glenashdale Burn far below. Above the path this impetuous stream leaps down a precipice in a fine waterfall.

2 Then the path widens and rises sharply through a plantation of conifers, from where goldcrests whisper. Finally you reach a row of steps. Climb these and then wind round on a few more steps and there is the magnificent viewing platform ahead of you. The sight is incredible, the sound tremendous. After pausing here, descend from the platform and continue upwards on the pleasing path to reach a bridge over the burn. Just above the bridge the burn descends in a series of fine peat-stained cascades and then the water collects itself before plunging down the rocks below. There is a single picnic table here.

3 Follow the distinct path onwards, progressing through tall conifers, which cut out the light from the forest floor. Go over a culverted tributary and carry on through the dark trees to go

over a bridge. Pass through a wall and carry on by the site of an iron-age fort. Cross another bridge over a second tributary, where you should pause to view, left, a wonderful waterfall upstream. Climb steps and walk on to two waymarks. The right-hand one directs you to the viewpoint, on your right, close to the edge of the gorge. From here you can sit on a seat, or stand, to look across the great ravine to see the main falls again – a great wide, slash of white foaming water.

4 After enjoying the view you should then take heed of the left-hand waymark. This one directs you back up through the trees, bearing steadily half right above the path you used to approach the viewpoint. You should on no account go on down through the forest. This waymarked path winds on steadily up, to arrive at a forest track, where you turn right for Whiting Bay. Descend the good track, which goes gently down through the forest. Where the trees open out, walk a wider airy track. Eventually cross a racing burn on large sturdy stepping stones, which should only present trouble if the burn is in spate and the stones are under water. Half way across the stones, look up left to see another great waterfall.

Gorse

5 Then go through a kissing gate and carry on, the way lined with flowering gorse. Go through the next gate and stroll on to go over crossroads. Continue on down, the road now lined with houses, to reach the A-road. Turn right and walk back through the attractive village to cross the bridge over the Glenashdale Burn to return to the parking place.

Practicals

Type of walk: Good footpaths and tracks to a magnificent waterfall. Very satisfactory.

Total distance:	3 miles/5km
Time:	3 hours
Maps:	OS Explorer 361/Landranger 69

8

Giants' Graves

Park and start the walk as for walk 7, grid ref 048253.

The Giants' Graves (two together) lie in a sun-filled clearing sheltered from the prevailing winds by dense conifers. These are chambered tombs and they were believed to have been constructed between 3,500 and 2,200 BC. A number of individuals would have been interred here before the grave was blocked up and covered with a great cairn of stones. They are now roofless and lie in ruins. Each tomb has two large upright stones at one end which were probably part of the entrance. How were they levered into position and embedded in the ground so securely that 4,000 years later they are still standing?

Giants' Graves

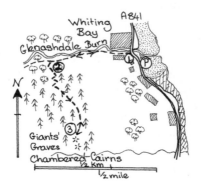

Walk 8

1 From the parking area in the layby beside the bus stop, on the shore side at the south end of Whiting Bay, cross the road and take the road, signposted 'Glenashdale Falls and Giants' Graves'. Continue ahead where the road becomes a track and go on until you can pass through a gate into a Forestry Commission (FC) planting. Walk on along the pleasing rising way through deciduous woodland until you reach a signpost, directing you sharp left to the Giants' Graves.

2 Then begin to climb a 'staircase' of over 250 steps through the forest. Take lots of pauses as you go, perhaps standing quietly in the hopes of seeing a red squirrel. As you near the top, look

Red squirrel

through the gaps in the trees, to see the ground sloping almost sheer downhill to Whiting Bay, and also superb views of the sea, sandy bays, and Holy Isle.

3 Follow the path as it emerges into a clearing containing the remains of the chambered cairns. Here bracken, rowan and flowering grasses fill the spaces between the graves and other interesting stones. Then begin your return by retracing your outward route rather than following any of the unmade routes from the back of the Giants Graves area – this is a recommendation from the FC.

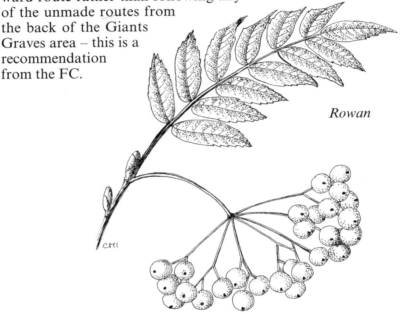

Rowan

Practicals

Type of walk: It is often suggested that you tack this walk onto the Glenashdale Falls walk but after climbing the innumerable steps better to make it a single walk. Once in the clearing it is a delectable place to be.

Total distance: 2 miles/3.4km
Time: 1–2 hours
Maps: OS Explorer 361/Landranger 69

9

Eas Mor Waterfall and Loch Garbad

Eas Mor

Park in the car park, grid 019217, on the north side of the A841, opposite the road down to Kildonan, nearly 5 miles east of Lagg.

Eas Mor waterfall tumbles 98ft/30m into a rock basin in Auchenhew Glen. It plummets over a superb amphitheatre of rock, which appears unexpectedly and magnificently as you climb up through the glorious deciduous woodland. It is said that sailors have used the rainbow that sometimes flickers over the descending water as a landmark.

1 Leave the back of the car park to walk the well reinforced, gently climbing track, lined with bushes and trees which, in spring, resound with the calls of willow warblers. Also in spring bluebells and wild garlic thrive along the edges. Follow the track as it winds right and comes beside an enormously deep ravine – so

deep that you cannot see the Allt Mor at its foot. Soon, through a gap in the trees, you have your first glimpse of the Eas Mor waterfall, which drops for a great depth in one long plume, down the cliff face on the far side of the ravine. A little further on is a viewing station, but take great care here, especially with youngsters, as there is little protection from the great drop.

2 Carry on to reach a sign that directs you left towards 'Loch Garbad 1 mile'. Stroll on along the good path, with conifers to the left and gorse-clad rolling pastures to the right, through which flow several little streams hurrying on their way to add their water to the waterfall. Eventually the path brings you to a gate, a stile, and a dog-gate, to the right side of the path, which you ignore. Keep on the easy path as it enters into conifer woodland with a small stream to your right. The path continues to rise steadily all the way. Step across a little stream beyond which the conifers lie back from the

Walk 9

path and great cushions of heather thrive. And then the loch is reached, a charming oval body of water, with conifers all round. There is a picnic table where you will want to take a break and enjoy the peace of this delightful corner.

3 Return back through the forest to reach the gate, the stile, and the dog gate, now on your left. Here you can choose your return route. Some walkers will wish to go past the waterfall once again and walk on to the car park. Others might wish to lengthen the walk by passing through the gate to step across a small stream. Then follow the track as it winds away left, across the pasture, continuing to a farm gate, where you go through a small gate beside it. Beyond, walk the ongoing track, heavily marked with

40

tractor wheels, beside a wall on the right. Curve round the corner and go through another small gate to the left of a farm gate and carry on between the outbuildings and the farmhouse, Ballymeanochglen. Stroll down the hedged access track, where marsh marigolds colour the ditch, and follow the track where it turns left, and then right, to descend to the A-road, here narrow and twisting.

4 Turn right along it, keeping well to the right side and listening for oncoming traffic. Go over the first bridge, continue round a big bend and then on down to a second burn. Here take a track on the right just before the bridge and walk up by the burn to a footbridge (currently under construction). Cross and climb the zigzagging path on the far side and then contour left through delightful woodland above the A-road to return to the car park.

Blackcap

Practicals

Type of walk: A most satisfactory ramble but take care when returning along the narrow short section of the A841.

Total distance: 3 miles/5km or 4 miles/6.5km
Time: 2 hours/3 hours
Maps: OS Explorer 361/Landranger 69

10

Black Cave, Bennan Head

Park opposite Kildonan shop and post office, grid ref 018212. The owner asks you to park tidily on the shore side of the open area. To reach this, turn south off the A841, down the narrow road to the village. Where the road turns left, drive right along the track to reach the excellent provision store.

Black Cave, Bennan Head

The roof of the **Black Cave on Bennan Head** is very high and most dramatic. It has an exit at the back with a little path leading up the cliff behind but this is not to be recommended. Use tide tables to work out when access isn't possible, that is at high tide and for one hour each side.

Year after year **common seals** bask on the dykes of rock that run out into the sea forming tiny shallow bays. Some seals lie alone on well-rounded boulders or a female may share another rock with her pups. As the seals laze they seem like clay models, then a tail swings into the air or a pup nudges its parent and you know that they are real. In some parts of Arran, clay seals have been placed on rocks just off shore.

1 Leave the parking area and walk west. Just beyond the last dwelling, look for a fine waterfall tumbling over a cliff face. Walk on along the delightful path that continues over a grassy raised beach. To your right rear magnificent cliffs covered with fine trees and low-growing vegetation. After a quarter of a mile, and if the tide is low, you reach the small bays, created by the rock dykes running out to sea, where you might see as many as fifty common seals. Just beyond look for another huge waterfall leaping in long white strands and then racing across the raised beach to the sea.

2 Continue along the shore, past more waterfalls, the path going over grass and pebbly shore for about a mile. The way then becomes more rocky and the path ceases and for half a mile the walker has to scramble over rocks and boulders that are easier to clamber over than they seem. Do

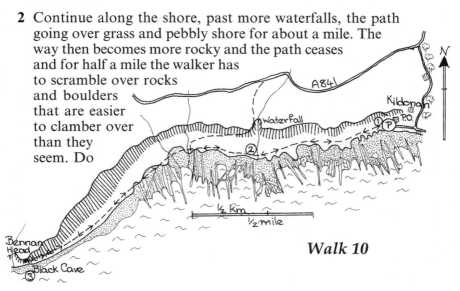

Walk 10

43

Common seal

not go too high up the slope because it is easier to make progress just at the top of the shore. Soon the boulders become larger but they are not so rough or jagged and there always seems to be a fairly easy way over them. And then your way appears to be barred by the cliff face, with the low tide sometimes lapping at its base. Here keep low, only a few feet above the shallow water, climbing round on a narrow rocky ledge, using both hands to help your progress. There is a higher ledge but it is not so easy to get on or off. Both children and adults seem to enjoy the scramble.

3 Once you reach Black Cave you will wish to dawdle for awhile before starting your return when the distances do not seem quite so far or the rocks so arduous. Look out to sea as you walk to where, perhaps, the sun illuminates the columnar cliffs and light-house on Pladda and where Ailsa Craig seems to rise above a skirt of mist.

Practicals

Type of walk: To reach the cave is quite a challenge. The ledge would not be suitable in stormy conditions. If you haven't tide tables ask at the shop whether the tides are suitable. To walk the shore to the start of the rocks is superb; in spring the flowers, birds and seals are a delight.

Total distance:	To cave 4 miles/6.5km
	To the start of the rocks 2½ miles/4km
Time:	2–3 hours/1 hour
Maps:	OS Explorer 361/Landranger 69

Kilmory Round

Park at Kilmory Church, grid ref 963218. To reach this, if travelling east, take the first turning on the left after the Lagg Hotel and follow the narrow lane as it bears right. Travelling west, take the turn on the right after passing the Torrylin Creamery. It is signed to Kilmory church.

Carn Ban is a chambered tomb, dating back to the Neolithic period, 3500–2200 BC. It was built of great slabs of stone and several people would have been interred within before the grave was blocked up and covered with a large cairn of stones. It was exposed in 1902 when it was described as having been divided into four compartments. Inside were small fragments of burned

Kilmory Church

and unburnt bones and some stone tools. It is believed that there is a second burial chamber at the downward end of the cairn. To reach the cairn involves a long trek from a public road, using forest tracks, then a narrow path through clear-fell and finally through more forest. It is found in a delightful, sun-lit clearing deep in the forest – though this may have been cleared before the publication of this book.

1 Walk back along the narrow lane from the parking area at the church. Where the lane turns sharp left, walk right along a track. Cross Kilmory Water by a bridge and then as the track climbs and winds left you may prefer to take a grassy trod that leaves left and climbs the slope, cutting off the corner. It rejoins the track further up from where you should look back for a fine view of the church. Then the track divides into three and you need to take the one on the right, that goes on to a craft centre at Cloined. Follow the track between the house and the workshop and continue on the now grassy way. It is hedged with young beech and arched overhead by more mature beech. This is a great delight to walk and where the trees end at an area of clear-fell some walkers may wish to return.

2 Carry on along the track through the clear-fell, where some regeneration is occurring, and from where you have a pleasing

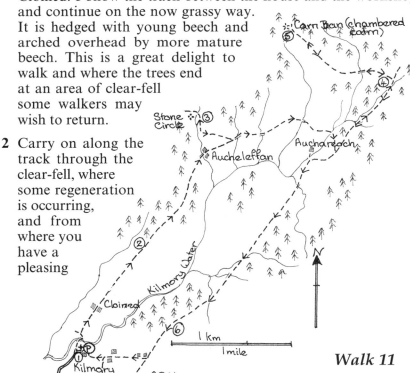

Walk 11

retrospective view of Ailsa Craig. Ignore a left turn and go on with conifers to the left and then move into conifer woodland, where the trees are set back from the track and heather and ferns line the way. After 1¼ miles/0.5km the track descends to the farmhouse at Aucheleffan and its duck pond. Once the farm was almost completely surrounded by conifers but now after considerable clear-felling the light comes flooding in. Continue on the track for approximately 400yds/430m to take a narrower forest track, bearing off left and climbing up through the clear-fell. The way winds right and then left and, just beyond, you arrive at the stone circle. It consists of four short sturdy stones set in a damp mossy area, with large clumps of heather growing around it. This is a lovely corner where you will want to pause.

3 Return down the hill and turn left on reaching the main track. Go past a pleasing waterfall on the right and then through more clear-fell, with fine views down right to Auchareoch set amid green pastures, a tiny green oasis in this huge forest. The track takes you over two more tumbling burns, and then after just over 1 mile/1.5km you reach a T-junction, where you turn left to climb the cycle way that crosses from the north of the island to the south (Whiting Bay/Lamlash). Go by a delightful planting of sycamore trees and continue past a long stretch of willow bushes that edge another burn and soften the sides of the track. Just beyond, turn left as directed by a signpost.

4 Walk ahead on a rising track until you reach its end at a turning circle from where you can see Sanda Island off the Mull of Kintyre and also Ireland – a faint smudge on the horizon. Look ahead at the end of the track and notice, slightly right, a way-mark (rather obscured by vegetation) directing you along a narrow, raised, grassy path running right (north-west) through the clear-fell. Enter the forest and then walk ahead for a few steps. The path then moves a little right before carrying on. Here, the continuing grassy path has been blocked by many conifers blown down in the last gale. At the time of writing a faint, muddy path goes on ahead, parallel with grassy way, and is marked with loops of orienteering tape. Eventually this rather slippery route rejoins the original trod and leads you on into the pleasing clearing and Carn Ban.

5 After spending time in the sun-filled hollow, return through the forest and along the green path that brings you to the turning circle. Then follow the forest road to the T-junction and walk right. Ignore the next right turn, walked earlier, and go ahead towards Kilmory as directed by the signpost. The track takes you well above Auchareoch farm where there are Highland cattle. It continues as a hedged track, a floral highway in spring, and then it climbs uphill, with heather moorland stretching away to the left, where you might spot a hen harrier quartering the vegetation. Eventually you reach the edge of the forest, where there is a signpost and an interesting plaque. From here there are extensive views over green pastures to Kilmory Church and out to sea. You are now over 2 miles/3.5km from Achareoch.

Hen harrier

6 Stroll on and when you can see traffic on the coast road and just beyond what looks like a standing stone (but is probably a gatepost) turn right to walk a pleasant track. Go past Dell Cottage and stride on ahead where the track becomes grassy and passes deep between hedgerows. It soon joins an unmade road and carries on ahead. Where the road swings away left, descend ahead, another hedged and grassy track to return to where you have parked at the church.

Practicals

Type of walk: A long generally sheltered walk, almost all on forest tracks, ideal for a windy day.

Total distance:	10 miles/16km
Time:	5–6 hours
Maps:	OS Explorer 361/Landranger 69

12

Torrylin Cairn, Kilmory

Park at the top of the hill on the A841, above and east of Lagg Hotel, grid ref 956216. The parking area lies to the side of the village hall.

The **Torrylin Cairn** is the much disturbed remains of a Neolithic chambered tomb used for family burials over a long period, approximately 5300 years ago. It shows the common characteristic of other burial tombs on Arran of a forecourt with an upright stone facade from which a rectangular burial chamber would be directly entered. This consisted of a passage divided

Torrylin Cairn

into four compartments, roofed with stone slabs. When excavated around 1900 the remains of at least six adults, a child, and an infant were found. Burials were usually collections of defleshed unburnt bones. It is thought that the bodies were first exposed on timber platforms. The bones were then placed in the tomb with the objects concerned with burial rituals such as feasting. The forecourt acted as a focus for these rituals.

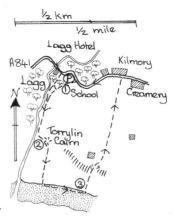

Walk 12

1 From the parking area at the side of the hall, walk round the front of the building to join a reinforced path that leads into deciduous woodland. Follow the easy way, which is suitable for wheelchairs users, as it continues, in spring, on its flower-lined way. Go with it as it curves right and then left to join another good path ascending gently from the foot of the hill. Carry on, left, soon to walk through bluebell woodland, high above a superb ravine, through which flows the Kilmory Water as it surges on its way to the shore. Stroll the delightful way as it moves out of the trees, mainly beech, into open pastures, with a wall to your left. Very soon take a gate, on the left, into the site of the cairn.

Siskin

2 After spending time in the well cared enclosure, leave by the gate and turn left to walk along the continuing path to descend a little. Pass through a 'wriggle' on the right, part of the 'Arran Coastal Way'. Cross the pasture to the far left corner. Climb the stile, which gives access to a stony beach, with pleasing golden sand lower down the shore. Go on ahead (left) soon to pass the Coastal Way shelter, ideal for a picnic and for bird watching –

look for oystercatchers, ringed plover and shelduck. Continue on a short way until you reach a huge boulder with a concrete wall added to its top – a good shelter for animals.

3 Turn left to walk a fine hedged track towards a boarded-up farmhouse. At the track end, turn left to return to the parking area. Or if you wish to visit the Torrylin Creamery to purchase a traditional hand-made Arran Dunlop cheese, turn right and then return, left, to the village hall parking area.

Bluebells

Practicals

Type of walk: Short and delightful.

Total distance: 1½ miles/2.5km
Time: 1 hour
Maps: OS Explorer 361/Landranger 69

13

Corriecravie Shore and Torr a'Chaisteil

Park in a largish space where there are children's swings opposite the name sign for the hamlet of Corriecravie, grid ref 916237. The hamlet lies between Blackwaterfoot and Sliddery, on the A841, on the south-west side of the island.

Torr a'Chasteil is one of several fortified enclosures constructed on Arran in the early centuries AD. On the OS map they are denoted as forts or duns. They were sometimes 40–50ft/10–15m across and surrounded by a thick drystone wall. Often they stood on a steep-sided hill as at Dun Fionn (see walk 1), King's Cross Point (see walk 6) and Drumadoon – a much larger fort (see walk 16). The dun, a defended farmstead, was sited close to agricultural land and with access to coastal resources. The farmhouse might have been constructed of timber, its roof resting on the walls of the dun. An 'outwork' cut off the promontory on which the fort stood to provide extra defence. Excavations done in the 19th century recovered human

Torr a'Chaisteil

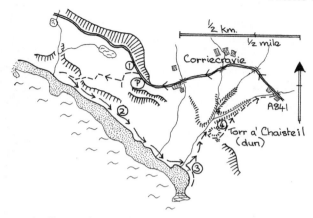

bones, a grinding stone, quern and pieces of haematite, and a midden providing evidence that this was a settlement.

1 Walk north-west from the parking area and, after a few steps along the A-road, take a good track, left, descending through gorse, to a reach a stile on the right. Beyond, stroll a grassy track through more gorse, with pasture on either side, to pass through a kissing gate. Descend the continuing track to the shore, where it ends at a cattle feeding station. Avoid the mud and carry on, left, along the beach using a sketchy path that is edged with yellow irises. Out to sea look for curious common seals, eider, and maybe a whimbrel on migration. Then the little path becomes easier to walk and in a short distance boulders force you up along a track, which heads to a gate. Beyond this is a patch of hawthorn bushes between you and the shore. From here you can see the Mull of Kintyre, spoon-shaped Sanda island and Ailsa Craig.

2 Carry on along a wet area where you need to step, with care, from boulder to boulder, or grassy tuft to grassy tuft. Pick your way onwards soon to reach a shingly drier area to approach a gate in a wire fence. Do **not** pass through but turn right towards the shore and wind round the end of the fence. Beyond in the gently swaying reeds you might hear the 'scratching' call of a sedge warbler. Go on ahead with a derelict wall and a fence to the left and the sea to your right to come to a small bay. Cross a little burn flowing out to sea and then pass through a gate in the fence on the left.

3 Walk ahead across a pasture towards the looming hill fort of Torr a'Chaisteil. Go through a gate and in a few steps wind right on a wide delightful grassy track that curves round between the foot of the hill and the peaked 'outwork'. Continue on to reach an interesting plaque. From here follow the little path, left, that takes you up, easily, to the top of the dun from where there is an exciting and extensive view.

Sedge warbler

4 Return to the track and walk ahead away from the dun towards the village, following the clear straight track that runs along the edge of a lovely ravine lined with deciduous trees and through which flows the hurrying burn, crossed on the shore. At one point the track becomes rather wet where you should keep to the rim of the ravine. Carry on ahead to pass through a kissing gate into a garden which you cross. Go up a bank to the right of the garden gate and over a stepped stile onto the A-road. Turn left and carry on through the hamlet to the parking area.

Practicals

Type of walk: A great shore route for those who do not mind getting their boots a little muddy. The dun on its hill is a pleasing climb and very interesting.

Total distance: 3 miles/5km
Time: 2½ hours
Maps: OS Explorer 361/Landranger 69

Kilpatrick Cashel

Park in the small walled area on the east side of the road, 1¼ miles/2km south of Blackwaterfoot, grid ref 903268. Look for the large 'Ancient Monument' sign.

Neolithic and Bronze-age remains were revealed when the site was last excavated. It is believed to be at least 4,000 years old and was a collection of stone lined graves. Today you can see a low turf and stone bank surrounding a vast green area of about three acres. Look for double walls and standing stones, and ridge and furrow marks on the turf. Conifers shelter the site on three sides, but they stand well back. The view is magnificent of Kintyre, Ireland in the distance, and away to the north the large mass of Beinn Bharrain. Today the cashel overlooks cultivated fields, which stretch to Blackwaterfoot.

Kilpatrick Cashel

Willow warbler

1 Leave the car park, left, and walk up beside a house, on your right, towards Kilpatrick farm, for 50yds/45m, to reach a tall black and white painted post. Here walk right. You are usually directed this way by an arrow on the post, but at the time of writing, it lies on the ground. Walk a short track, partly reinforced and fenced on one side, to come to a gate and a fine stepped and gated stile. Beyond, walk on along the grassy track, with rushy pastures on either side. Away to your left, almost hidden by dense low vegetation and pleasing ash trees, hurries the Allt a' Ghoirtean. Follow the path to the next black and white post, with an arrow directing you half left towards the next post. Go through a gate and carry on as directed by another post.

2 Just beyond, at a muddy Y-junction, take the left-hand branch to climb uphill where the path soon improves. The posts lead you up through the rough grass of the moorland and then, suddenly, you come upon the huge area of green turf, a wonderful sight among the tawny rough grass.

3 After you have explored this delightful site, return the same way.

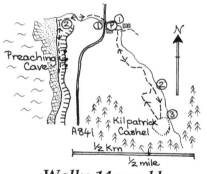

Walks 14a and b

Practicals

Type of walk: Easy and short. The way can be muddy in parts but the site, when reached, is well worth the effort.

Total distance: 2 miles/3.4km
Time: 1 hour
Maps: OS Explorer 361/Landranger 69

Kilpatrick Cave or Preaching Cave

Park as for walk 14a.

The cave is named after the hermit Patrick. It was once used as the parish school and also for religious services. In the 19th century it provided a **meeting place for those fanatics** who wanted a fervent priest to replace the milder man presented by the 9th Duke of Hamilton. Around the cave grow dense bracken, golden rod and ling, and among the pebbles, flourish pink persicaria, burdock and sorrel.

1 Cross the road from the little car park and go through a gate on the north side of the Allt a' Ghoirtean. Walk ahead over a wide

Preaching Cave

grassy area between scrubby hawthorns to where the burn swings across the path. Wade or step across and walk on to an awkward gate in the fence on the edge of the shore. Here, look for curlews and oystercatchers.

2 Turn left and walk along the springy turf path that runs just above the pebbled beach. After a quarter of a mile the cliffs are higher and under great rocky overhangs are several caves. One small cave has a smaller one above it. Then comes Kikpatrick Cave. Return the same way, enjoying the view of Kilpatrick Point.

Curlew

Practicals

Type of walk: Short, easy and level

Total distance:	1 mile/1.5km
Time:	30 minutes
Maps:	OS Explorer 361/Landranger 69

15

Ballygown Fort

The **Iron-Age Ballygown fort** lies on the summit of Cnoc Ballygown, 686ft/226m. There is very little evidence of a hill fort to be seen, but you may be able to trace the ramparts. What a wonderful site it must have been for spotting an enemy approaching by sea or land. There is a very good view of Machrie Moor.

Park in front of the telecom building on the B880 at grid ref 908294. This lies just over ½ mile/1km south of Shiskine.

1 Walk back a few steps in the direction of Shiskine and cross the road to take the rough track that ascends to Balgowan farm. Go through the gate on the left, just before the farm buildings, and curve round left and then right, with the farm buildings to your right. Go through another gate and walk left up the continuing

Walk 15

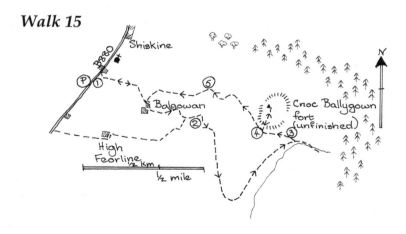

Shiskine church

track, through a pasture. Follow the track as it bears right, with Ben Nuis coming into view, and then wind left following the 'Arran Access Trust' waymark, directing you on up the track, with beech trees lining the field boundary. Follow the now grassy track right, and soon, left. From here you can look across to Kintyre and down on the wide apron of good agricultural land that stretches across to the shore and is dotted with farmhouses.

2 Wind round with the track through hillocks covered with gorse to pass through a waymarked gate in a fence – where you might spot stonechats sitting on the fence wire. Go along the right hand track, climbing through more banks of gorse and continue on. Pass through the next waymarked gate and go ahead over a large field. Once through the next gate you are out onto moorland and the path leads you left, climbing steadily to pass through another gate. Carry on gently uphill, with a fence to your left and on reaching a signpost, turn left for Ballygown fort.

3 Climb the slope and continue on a grassy swathe where there is a waymark. Go on to pass a signpost with 'alternative route of descent' on it. Just beyond, the way divides. To reach the top, go straight up. The cairn lies just beyond a fence with a hurdle gate. Pause here to admire the extensive view.

4 Return to the signpost and follow the direction for the alternative route and stroll, right, round below the hill. Carry on as directed by a waymark, along a wide green swathe. Look for the rampart as you go down. Follow the way until it reaches a steepish, wide dirt track, which you descend. At its foot the track winds a short way, left, to a gate into a pasture and a clump of

gorse. Beyond walk left, descending gently along a faint but wide grassy trod that soon passes through more gorse. It is easy to follow as it descends to a T-junction. Here turn, right, and walk along a track – don't be worried when the track climbs gently before beginning to descend, quite steeply down to a gate.

5 Once through bear left across a pasture to a grassy 'valley' between low hillocks. Drop down the valley and descend to a gate between two fine beech trees. Walk down beside more trees, on your right and, at the boundary ahead, turn left and walk towards the farm once more. Go through a gate close to the outbuildings, taken earlier, and in a few steps go through the gate on the right, onto to the track, ascended at the start of the walk. Turn right to descend to the road and then left to where you have parked. As you go look for the fine Shiskine parish church, built of red stone and splendidly red against the bright green pastures.

Stonechat CH

Practicals

Type of walk: This is a glorious walk. The route sounds complicated but it is fairly well waymarked and you just keep going on up, or down.

Total distance:	3 miles/5km
Time:	2 hours
Map:	OS Explorer 361/Landranger 69

16

Drumadoon Point and the Doon

Park at the public car park by the golf course at Blackwaterfoot, grid ref 895282. This is reached by a right turn, at the bottom of the hill, where the A841 turns left towards the harbour and the Kinloch Hotel. The golf course is well signposted.

The **Doon or fort** is believed to be Iron-Age and about 2,000 years old. It is D-shaped and stands on the headland of Drumadoon and possibly gave refuge to a tribal community. There is little to see on this 12-acre hilltop area except for traces of a circular wall, probably part of an ancient rampart. The huge mound is covered with flowering grasses, harebells and tormentil. The view from the top is superb, across the Kilbrannan Sound to much of Kintyre. It must have been a wonderful site for observing invaders. It is defended on the seaward side by spectacular perpendicular columns of basalt and, to the landward side, stretches pastoral Arran overlooked by a solitary standing stone.

1 Walk on from the car park on a good farm road, with the sea to your left and the golf course to the right. After about 430yds/

The Doon, Drumadoon Point

400m, ignore a signpost directing you on along the track and inland. Instead follow a path, left, onto the shore. Cross the burn and walk on along the sands, where you might spot curlews and cormorants, with low 'stranded' cliffs and sand dunes to the right. In half a mile, wind round Drumadoon Point and carry on along a grassy path until you have to clamber over some rocks, below two huge rocky outcrops, to reach the tip of the golf course. Walk up beside the fence, on your left, and then climb a stile over it. Turn right and walk a short way up beside the fence in the direction of a magnificent rock pinnacle. Follow the path as it bears left, right up against the base of the columnar cliffs. Here you might spot fulmars nesting high above you. This is a narrow path and it is exposed in parts so care should be taken.

Walk 16

The Doon

N

½ km

½ mile

Golf Course

A841

Drumadoon Point

Blackwaterfoot

2 At the end of the superb rock columns, join the path coming south from the King's Cave and bear right up the slope to reach a waymark. Wind right and continue on to go through a gate. A little way along look for a narrow grassy trod ascending an easy slope on the right. Pass through the ancient rock wall of the fort and walk left, to pass a single standing stone. Follow a wide grassy trod that continues pleasingly along the side of the Doon and then bear right, up a little path, to the highest point, from where the views are superb. If you do move over to the cliff edge, proceed with care. Then return down the narrow path and retrace part of your outward route along the wide grassy trod, to a gap in the tiny wall. Go through and down an easily

Fulmar

descending path to join a wider way. Turn right and walk on to climb a stile, waymarked with the coastal path logo on the far side.

3 Walk ahead for a few steps to join a reinforced track at the side of the golf course. A waymark directs you left. Follow the track and also where it curves right between the greens of the golf course, keeping a wary eye for golf balls, to come to the signpost ignored almost at the outset of your walk. Continue on bearing steadily left to return to the car park.

NB If the thought of walking the narrow path below the columns of rock is not for you, then take the signposted track inland (see second and third line of point 1) walking through the golf course to the stile. Beyond, follow any of the narrow paths that slope across the pasture, left, to ascend to the fort.

Tormentil

Practicals

Type of walk: Good tracks and paths. It would be a pity not to see the basalt columns even if you do not wish to walk the little path at their foot. To do this continue along the shore (not possible when the tide is very high) and wind round the Point from where you have a spectacular view. From here you might spot, much further along the shore, the Kings Cave (walk 17).

Total distance:	Circular walk 2½ miles/4km
	There and back by the same route
	1½ miles/2.5km
Time:	1½ hours and 1 hour
Maps:	OS Explorer 361/Landranger 69

17

King's Cave

Park in the Forestry Commision's car park, grid ref 897315. This lies south of Machrie and can be reached by driving south on the A841 over Machrie Bridge and through Tormore.

King's Cave,
Machrie

C.M. Isherwood

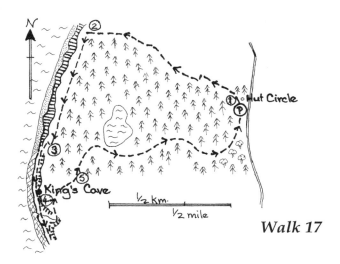

Walk 17

King's Cave is one of many caves on the rocky coast of Arran formed, thousands of years ago, by the action of the sea on the cliffs. In places the sea penetrated the soft sandstone to a depth of over 100ft/30m. King's Cave is reputed, but dismissed by others, to have been the hiding place of Robert the Bruce when he started his campaign to take the Scottish crown in 1314. Bruce who formed a guard of Arran men had a special affection for the island. The episode with the spider is believed to be a great legend. The cave may have been used as a chapel in the 5th century and, here, in the 18th century meetings of the Kirk Sessions were held. On the outside ledges of the cave, fulmars nest.

1 With your back to the A-road, walk right along the pleasing re-inforced path through the forest. As you emerge into the open, still with trees to your left. pause to look back over Machrie Moor sheltered by high hills. Carry on the undulating path with bright green moss edging the forest and stretching a little way into the trees. Soon, far below you, Machrie Bay comes into view, with white-topped waves breaking on the shore. Beyond, you can see Kintyre. Soon the path passes between banks of heather, with more heather covering the sloping pasture that drops away to your right. As you go you pass two seats well placed to enjoy the superb view.

2 Follow the path as it winds round left, with the sea to your right,

with more heather-covered slopes now descending very steeply to the sea, and you can just spot the tops of pine trees growing far below. Look for goldcrests in the trees to your left. The path rises and falls and the views out to sea are superb. Look for the spoon-shaped island of Sanda off the tip of Kintyre. Go on to pass another seat.

3 Continue on to pass a small railed area that leads you to the top of a long rocky gully, which you go down to reach the sea shore. It is naturally stepped for an easy descent and it is much more negotiable than it looks. The sides of the gully are clad, almost from the top to base, with lichen. At the foot of the ravine go through a gate and carry on, left, where you can choose to walk the grassy way or along the pebbly beach. To your left are little paths that lead through the vegetation to small caves. Go on along the shore until you reach a stepped path, climbing up to a huge cave, with very tall iron gates. Go through these into the fine high-topped cave. Straight ahead, and towards the back of the cave, is a large bluff of rock, with a blind-ended tunnel on either side. It is on this buttress of rock that faint carvings can be discerned. These possibly date from early Christian or Viking times. One carving is of a large cross standing in some sort of vegetation. The other, to its right, towards the top of the cross is a human figure holding, perhaps, a bow above its head.

4 Walk on from the gates of the cave to pass through a natural arch and then another huge cave. Leave by the far side of the latter and walk on along the continuing path, which soon begins to climb to a signpost. Take the left branch, the higher one, which climbs quite steeply. Follow the path as it winds round sharply and then arcs round a hillock before climbing again, up

Goldeneye

and up to the top of the cliffs. Stroll on along the path as it traverses the grassy top, with heather to your right stretching up to the hills and with King's Cave, unseen and far below you. Take care here if the wind is very strong. Then the path bears right and heads inland to go through two gates into the forest.

5 Walk on along the continuing good path, with no difficulty in finding your way. As you progress look out for a gap in the trees, on your left, to view a large lochan where goldeneye duck swim. Carry on along the path, which eventually brings you back to the car park, with its interesting information boards.

Goldcrest

Practicals

Type of walk: A delightful walk, with good paths for most of the way. The descent of the gully might present a problem for some. The path up onto the cliff tops, on your return, might be muddy after rain. Wear strong footwear and don't forget to take a torch.

Total distance: 3 miles/5km
Time: 2–3 hours
Maps: OS Explorer 361/Landranger 69

18

Machrie Circles

Park in the small parking area almost opposite the signed track to the stone circles, grid ref 895331. This lies on the A841, just south of the bridge over the Machrie Water. Take care not to block gates.

Stone circles may have been constructed for religious reasons, perhaps as calendars using the position of the sun and the moon, or as meeting places, but no one can be quite sure why they were built. They are believed to date back to Neolithic and the Bronze Age, some 5,500 to 3,000 years ago. In 1985–86 the remains of timber circles were found which predated two of the stone circles. It is believed that there are still many ancient sites such as

Standing Stones, Machrie Moor

houses, burial cairns, and field systems lying below the peat. This area of Arran has always attracted settlers. It is a triangular basin of the most fertile land on the island.

1 Cross the road from the parking area and climb the stile beside the gate. Walk ahead along a wide track to pass through pastures. Watch out here for nesting curlews at the right time of the year. Carry on along a fenced area with a copse of birch trees about Machrie Water. Follow the track as it turns sharp right between more pastures and climb a stile beside a gate. Beyond lies fenced Moss Farm Road granite stone circle. A stile gives access. This is thought to be another kerbed cairn (see Auchagallon Circle, walk 17a), where the huge granite stones formed a kerb round a large burial mound.

2 Return to the track and walk on the reinforced winding way. Just before the next gate, a narrow path leads left to a solitary stand-ing stone, which you might wish to visit. Then pass through the gate/stile and turn right to take the next stile and follow a grassy path to view several large stones, part of a chambered cairn. Return to the main path and carry on to a fine granite stone circle on a little hillock. From here look down towards a well-signed gate beside a derelict farmhouse and barn and then walk on, downhill, towards the gate. Beyond, to the right of the gate, are four large granite stones, each facing north, east, south and west. Further along the grassy path, to the left, stands a huge sandstone monolith, with smaller stones about it.

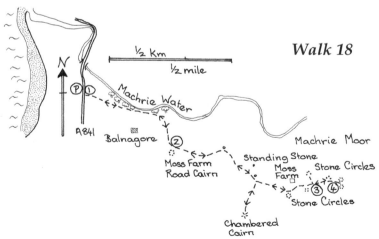

3 Again return to the path and carry on to view the 'famous three', the three spectacular sandstone standing stones, part of a circle. These will be well known to walkers as pictures of them adorn maps and many books. They glow warmly in the sunshine and stand against a wonderful backdrop of Machrie Moor and the northern mountains. They can be seen from the road across Machrie Moor and from Kilpatrick Dun.

4 Continue on the main path to reach another granite stone circle, then bear a little left to reach a smaller and final circle. Linger awhile among the stones, the bracken, and the heath spotted orchis, and think back in time. The surrounding hills, quiet and mist topped, must have appeared much the same when the stones were put in place – though probably with more trees about this extensive basin of land.

Heath Spotted Orchis

Practicals

Type of walk: Good reinforced tracks for much of the way, and then grassy paths. Level walk. Some interesting information boards to help you enjoy the site. Wheelchair occupants, with good pushers, should be able to reach Moss Farm Road circle. The gate at the start is not locked, just very heavy.

Total distance:	3 miles/5km
Time:	1 hour
Maps:	OS Explorer 361/Landranger 69

19a

Auchagallon Stone Circle

Park on a bare patch of ground beside the phone box and the little telephone exchange, Auchagallon, grid ref 892345. This parking area lies opposite the ancient monument sign for the circle and at the point where the Machrie Farm road leaves the A841 to join The String.

This **pleasing circle of red sandstone slabs**, 47ft/14m in diameter, has 15 stones surviving and dates back to the Bronze Age, about 4,000 years ago. Although it is known as a stone circle, it was possibly constructed as a kerbed cairn, with an almost continuous ring of sandstone blocks around it, many of which are now missing. It is believed that this type of cairn was erected to cover

Auchagallon Stone Circle

burials of important people. Nineteenth century excavations found a cist, a stone lined burial chamber. On the mound within and outside the stones, harebell, yarrow, and hawkbit thrive. In autumn look for red and yellow wax cap fungus.

1 Cross the road from the parking area and follow the ancient monument sign that directs you up a winding farm track. Very soon you reach the splendid circle, which lies just above the track.

Harebells

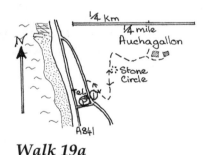

Walk 19a

Practicals

Type of walk: Short, easy climb

Total distance:	200yds/240m
Time:	10 minutes each way
Maps:	OS Explorer 361/Landranger 69

19b

Auchencar 'Druid' Stone

Park on the grassy flat that edges the shore at grid ref 889359. This lies close to the sign for the Old Byre, between Auchagallon and Dougarie.

The **Druid Stone** is named after the nearby farmhouse. It is a stark, white spectacular standing stone, to be found in the middle of a field. It is believed to have been erected around 3,000 to 4,000 years ago, during the Bronze Age. It is most impressive seen against the background of Ben Bharrain or from inland with the sea behind.

Standing Stone, Auchencar

1 Walk up the single track road, towards the farm, for just less than ½ mile/0.8km to take a stile over the fence, on the left, to walk the 110yds/100 metres to the stone. If you are visiting in spring, pause by the stone and listen for meadow pipits trilling their nuptial songs, quick repetitions of sharp notes as they ascend and float down with outspread wings.

Walk 19b

Meadow Pipit

Practicals

Type of walk: Level access road

Total distance: Less that 1 mile/1.5km
Time: 10 minutes each way
Maps: OS Explorer 361/Landranger 69

20

Dougarie, Two lochans, Sail Chalmadale and Loch Iorsa

Park in a wide parking area opposite the footpath signed Sail Chalmadale, grid ref 882370. To reach this travel north from Blackwaterfoot, on the A841, and look for the layby once you have crossed the bridge over the Iorsa Water, at Dougarie.

Just before you cross the bridge over the Iorsa Water, look right to see the stately **Dougarie Lodge**. It was built as a shooting lodge towards the end of the 19th century.

Loch Iorsa receives water from the lonely Glen Iorsa, which is enclosed by high hills including the two Beinn Tarsuinns, and also from Loch Tanna. A narrow boggy path of sorts continues from the boathouse and along the side of the loch but it is not to be recommended. Sit by the quiet water and enjoy the reflections and see if you can spot deer on the slopes of Beinn Choarach.

Loch Iorsa

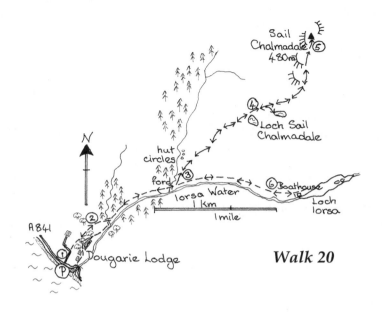

Walk 20

1 Take the signed and metalled track opposite the parking area, which is fenced and walled and passes through pastures full of sheep. Where the track swings left, ascend the large sandstone steps that climb up the stranded cliff. At the top, go over the stile on the right and continue on a distinct path to cross a fence by another stile. Follow the path through a grassy area with scattered trees and then step over a wire into sycamore and lime woodland. Leave the trees by stepping over more wire and continue on the good path through a more open area.

2 The way becomes boggy and then improves as you follow the black and white marker posts through the lush vegetation. Ahead you have a fine view of Ben Nuis and Ben Tarsuinn. Descend to a track and bear a little left to cross a sturdy footbridge over a tributary of the Iorsa, the Allt na h-Airighe. Carry on the now pleasing track that swings out into the U-shaped valley. To the right flows Iorsa Water, wide and surging, with many stone weirs across it to create deeper pools for the salmon. Go past a new planting of rowan and birch and then pass through a deer gate to walk on along the reinforced track to reach a concrete ford over another tributary of the Iorsa that flows through Glen Scaftigill. There once was a bridge but it was washed away during a storm. If the burn is in spate and you do not want to get your feet wet, you may be able to cross on large boulders higher upstream.

3 Immediately beyond, look for a grassy swathe that leaves the track, left, and continues roughly parallel with the burn, just crossed. Gradually the indistinct path moves away from the Scaftigill and after 100yds/90m or so, it divides (very difficult to spot) and you need the right branch. This path is narrow but soon becomes more obvious. It has been made by an all terrain vehicle (ATV) using a much earlier path that was easy to follow. The way goes on to climb two bluffs. Do not be tempted to make your own way over the purple moor grass, which grows in large ankle-wrenching tufts. When the path crosses heather, the plant often obliterates the way but keep on up, steadily heading north-east (half right). The ATV route continues for about ¾ mile/ 1.3km until suddenly you spot Loch Sail Chalmadale, an almost circular pool on the shoulder of Sail Chalmadale, where you might wish to take your first break.

4 Continue on the now distinct path as it starts to climb towards the overshadowing hill. A short way along, bear right to cross the very rough pasture to a nameless lochan, which is long and narrow, and hidden in its hollow. Then return to the path at the

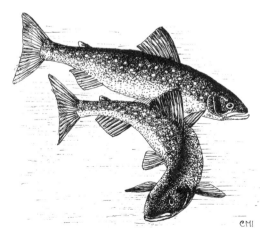

Salmon

foot of the hill. Here, if you wish to climb to the summit of Sail Chalmadale, follow the path, keeping to the right of some granite slabs where the path soon disappears. Go on up steeply over boulders and then the way eases and passes through heather and more boulders and there is a little path to the summit cairn at 1560ft/480m. You'll want to pause here to enjoy the superb view.

5 Return along the little path until it disappears. Take care on the steepish part and finally keep well left of the granite slabs to make your way back to the first loch. Make sure you pick up the path used for your ascent. Do not attempt to descend the path-less slopes – it is possible but it is just one very steep, long battle to avoid boggy patches, the ubiquitous tussock grass and then bracken. On reaching the main track through the glen, turn left and walk on for a mile. The track ends at the boathouse at the start of pleasing Loch Iorsa.

6 Return along the track, cross the Scaftigill by the concrete ford and on through the deer gate. Continue on to cross the foot-bridge and take the sign posted path, leading off right from the main track. Continue on to the road, where you have parked.

Practicals

Type of walk: A challenging climb to two mountain lochs, which is made most pleasurable if you spend a little time finding the narrow path. You may also be tempted to climb Sail Chalmadale before returning to the ATV path that takes you down to the Iorsa Water. The track to Loch Iorsa is easy to walk.

Distances:	6 miles/9.5km to the lochans
	8 miles/13km to the lochans and to Loch Iorsa
	9½ miles/15.1km to the lochans,
	Sail Chalmadale and Loch Iorsa
Time:	3–4 hours/4–5 hours/6 hours
Maps:	OS Explorer 361/Landranger 69

21

Imachar Caves and Shoreline

Park at the foot of Imachar Brae, on the sea side, in one of two laybys, grid ref 865402. This lies between Pirnmill and Machrie on the A841.

Cave at Imachar

The rocks on **Imachar beach** are of Cambrian schist, probably laid down 550 million years ago as a deposit of sea mud. This was subjected to high temperatures and pressure, as it lay buried, which brought about extensive folding, and veins of quartz were intruded into it. The shore above the beach is a raised beach.

Raised beaches were formed at the end of the last ice-age. As the ice melted sea levels rose and the beaches developed. Then, much more gradually, the land, which had been held down by the weight of the ice, rose, so that the beaches became 'stranded' well above the present sea level. The road round Arran runs on a raised beach (or wave-cut platform) for much of its way.

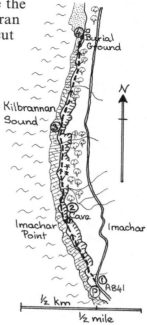

Walk 21

1 Walk on (north) from the layby along a grassy path, just above the beach. Cross a burn and climb the fence by a stile, which is tucked up behind bushes. Carry on along the path with the dramatic cliffs, where fulmars nest, and caves to your right; there is a small path to the latter, leading off right. Look out to sea as you go where you might spot eiders all year and great northern divers in winter. Curve round Imachar Point, clambering over a few rocks, but be aware that at very high tides these are under water. Beyond, cross a stream and look right to see a pretty waterfall, descending from the top of the cliffs, through willow scrub.

2 Continue on the very good path over grass (a useful picnic site) to come to three fine stacks, one with a perpendicular groove into which jackdaws enter and leave, busily tending their nests. Goldfinches flit about the bushes behind the huge structure. There are several more caves in the cliffs here, hidden by bracken and trees; the adventurous might wish to explore them using animal tracks to push through the dense vegetation. Go on to cross another stream and again look towards the cliffs to see its attractive descent in one long fall. At the next fence there isn't a stile, but the wire has been cut and you can step over it easily.

Goldfinch

3 Stroll on to round another small headland on rocks, which will also be under water at very high tides. Press on to come beside a broken fence. Here turn left to descend a little onto rocks Then carry on over the rocks, soon to join a grassy area, with a pebble beach and patches of sand away to your left. Go over the top of the beach. Look right to see a huge heap of granite boulders, with a metal cross beyond it. Go right up to the top of the beach and round behind the granite into a little graveyard. Inside among flags, grow tall meadow sweet, woundwort and ferns. Here a robin sings a melancholy song. Many of the gravestones bear inscriptions to many of the McMillen family.

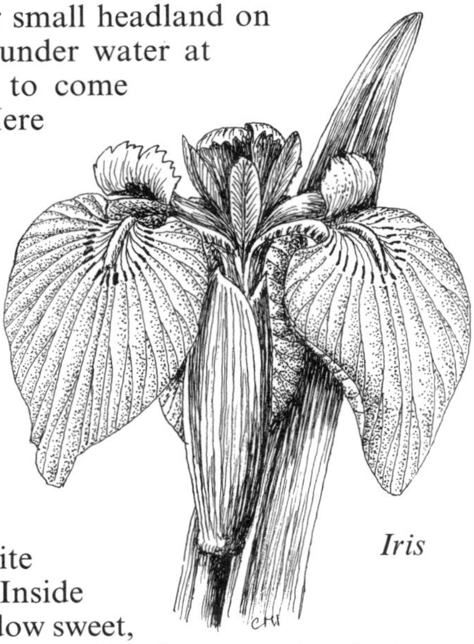

Iris

4 After a pause here in this quiet corner, return along the same path.

Practicals

Type of walk: A lovely, dramatic walk. Remember to check the tides.

Total distance:	3 miles/5km
Time:	3 hours
Maps:	OS Explorer 361/Landranger 69

Beinn Bharrain

Park in a layby on the shore side at Mid Thundergay, grid ref 879467. The hamlet lies on the east side of the A841, between Catacol and Pirnmill, on the west coast of Arran

Some of **Arran Gaelic place names** can be daunting, but are apt. For example: Coire Fhionn Lochan – the corrie with the little white, or fair, or pale loch; Meall Donn – the brown hill; Meall Bhig – little hill: Beinn Bhreac – the dappled hill; Mullach Buidhe, the highest top, means yellow hill.

Coire Fhionn Lochan (Corrie Lochan) is nearly round and about ¼ mile/0.5km across. It lies, at about a 1000ft/306m, in a hollow scooped out by a glacier at the end of the last ice-age. It has three beaches of coarse granite sand, the water is gloriously clear and many enjoy swimming in it.

Pirnmill is named after the pirns or bobbins that were made here. Look behind the Lighthouse café to see the former bobbin mill.

Coire Fhionn Lochan

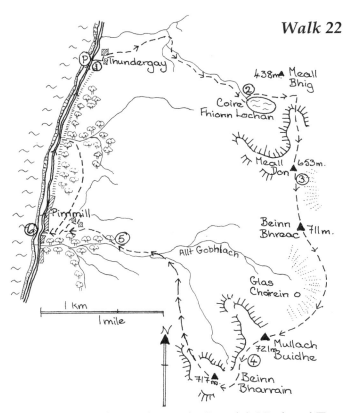

All the high granite peaks are in Scottish National Trust terri-tory and so can be walked at any time of the year. But Beinn Bharrain is not, nor are the Catacol Hills. Culling of deer occurs between August and February and if you intend to walk at this time make sure you use the **Hillphones service**, which provides recorded messages detailing where stalkers are operating day-to-day so that these area can be avoided. For information tel 01770 302363.

1 At Mid Thundergay climb the track signposted 'Footpath Corrie Lochan 2'. to a gate into a pasture and then climb steadily to go through the gate in the deer fence. Continue on to cross the Lenimore Burn on stepping stones. Follow the path as it turns right and continues to rise through bracken. Step across the burn that flows out of the loch and begin to climb up beside it. Ascend the path up through heather until you reach the lochan in its hollow scooped out by a glacier.

2 Follow the path to the north (left) of the lochan and then begin the climb to the col between Meall Bhig (1430ft/438m) and Meall Donn (2115ft/653m). Here look for the path bearing right and begin the climb up the steep slope of Meall Donn. To the right you can look down into Coire Lochan.

3 After losing some height, begin the steady climb to the cairn on Beinn Bhreac (2333ft/711m). Pause here to enjoy the spectacular view over The Castles (Sleeping Warrior), A Chir, Cir Mhor and Goatfell. Drop down again to walk along the shoulder above Glas Choirein. Look down into the hollow to see a tiny lochan. This corrie is the favourite haunt of deer. Then begin the long but easy climb to the trig point (2367ft/721m) on Mullach Buidhe. (Stretching north-west from here is a "Striding Edge" ridge which you should avoid.)

4 Follow the clear path downhill to cross the shoulder. Begin the steep short climb to Beinn Bharrain, the summit a tumble of granite boulders (2353ft/ 717m). From now on the way takes you gently down. Cross a wide grassy area and bear steadily right to Eagle Crag. Follow the path through boulders down the gentle well-defined ridge, leading north-west. This takes you safely to the open moorland, which is quite wet at first. Strike ahead to

Red deer hinds

pick up a drier sheep track that leads to the side of the hurrying Allt Ghoblach (the forked burn). Cross at an easy place, where some boulder hopping is required, and climb up to a good path. Turn left, downstream, and walk beside the lovely tree-lined burn. Follow the path as it swings right across rough grass to descend to the side of a small tributary burn. Step across, climb left up the bank and continue descending.

5 Head for the gate in the deer fence, close to the edge of the gorge. Walk ahead to cross the next deer fence, close to the burn. Continue through pleasing birch woodland to climb another stile. A clear path continues, bearing steadily right to a further stile out of the trees. Join the farm track and walk left into Pirnmill.

6 To rejoin your car, turn right on the A-road and walk the usually quiet road for 1½ miles/2.5km

Mountain Everlasting

Practicals

Type of walk: A pleasing, fairly easy trek to what many think is the prettiest lochan on Arran. The walk along the ridge to Beinn Bharrain is on a clear path and provides good dry walking. The moorland path can be boggy but the final path to Pirnmill is dry.

Total distances: To the lochan and back 3 miles/5km
The full walk 9 miles/14.5km
Time: 2 hours and 5–6 hours
Maps: OS Explorer 361/Landranger 69

23

Catacol, Lochan a' Mhill

Leave your vehicle at the small signed car park on the A841, south of Catacol's 'Twelve Apostles' and south of Catacol Bridge, grid ref 910489. This lies close to a large white house, Fairhaven, offering accommodation.

Lochan a' Mhill lies in a lovely, lonely hollow in the hills, overshadowed by Meall nan Damh on its right (west) side. **The Twelve Apostles** are twelve almost identical houses. They were built around the 1860s to rehouse the people who lived in Glen Catacol when they were 'cleared' to make way for deer, which provided more money for the landowners than sheep.

Lochan a' Mhill

1 Leave the back of the car park by a reinforced track to walk beside the Catacol river on your left. The path soon becomes grassy as it passes through an open area with scattered birch. Go through a deer gate and cross the Allt nan Eireannach on boulders and then head across a field to the right corner of a camping barn used by young people.

2 Step into the deciduous woodland behind the barn to climb a faint often wet path, keeping parallel with the burn just crossed. The way is boggy to start with and by the middle of June it will be almost impassable because of the rampant bracken that can grow to over

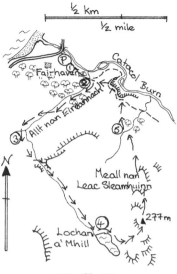

Walk 23

head height. Persevere up the tiny path and over the sweet-smelling bog myrtle to pass under some very tall deciduous trees, keeping a little way from the edge of the deep tree-lined ravine through which tumbles the burn. Then move out onto open moorland using a rather wet path, with the steep slopes of Creagan nan Gobhar to your left. Very soon the indistinct path drops down a little to the side of the burn which, at this point, you can step across. Go straight ahead, up the slope, to join a better path and walk left. Here you might spot or hear the red

Red grouse in heather

grouse. Where the path divides, take the left-hand branch and drop down a short way to re-cross the burn, on stones, just beyond the confluence of the Eireannach and the stream descending from Lochan a' Mhill.

3 Keep beside stream and right of an ancient fence, using a faint path. Wind round right of a hillock and then move left closer to the stream once more. Pass under birch and rowan on a better path to a place where you can step over the cascading burn. Then climb a distinct path, keeping the rock face of Creagan nan Gobhar on your left. Carry on along the little path as it bears slightly right across a boggy col and then ascend with it up the left side of a shallow ravine through which the stream descends between scattered rowan and birch. Continue up the path through heather until you reach the brow. From here you have a dramatic sighting of the jagged tops of A'Chir to the right, between more remote tops, and of the Castles to the left of the other distant tops. A little below you is the lovely little Lochan a' Mhill and if the midges are absent this is the place to have your break.

4 From the side of the pool you can see Gleann Diomhan ahead and to the right the great cleft of Glen Catacol. After a pause here, walk a quarter of the way, clockwise, round the lochan and then climb, left up the easy slope to the ridge of Meall nan Leac Sleamhuinn. Turn left along the ridge to reach the highest point at 900ft/272m, from where there are fine views of Catacol. You might spot deer here. Leave the top by its steepish slope, heading

Bog myrtle

towards Catacol, passing over often wet tussock grass and short heather. Descend carefully aiming for a little stream that drains the slope, crossing it as near the valley bottom as you can manage.

5 Once across use animal tracks through the heather gradually descending to the wettish floor of the valley. Step across the wet patches and round the pools, heading for an obvious path that continues round the rim of a crag edge below which curves the Catacol River. Follow the good path until you reach the camping field once more. Take the path that crosses diagonally to where you crossed the Eireannach early on in the walk. Go through the deer gate and return to the car park.

Purple Moor Grass

Practicals

Type of walk: This is a challenging walk for seasoned fell walkers, who can cope with wet paths or the lack of paths. But the rewards are great, fine views and the hills all to yourselves. Bracken can be tedious on the first part of the ramble, so plan your walk before it starts to rampage or after it has died down.

Total distance: 3 miles/5km
Time: 3 hours
Maps: OS Explorer 361/Landranger 69

24

Catacol, Glen Diomhan, Beinn Tarsuinn – the second!

Park at Catacol Bridge, grid ref 910489, as for walk 23.

If travelling north from Brodick, on one's first visit to the Isle of Arran, the countryside appears very wild, and it seems unbelievable that all the land is owned and managed. Dairy farming is important along the fertile coastal belt. Sheep and cattle are reared on higher grassland and heather moorland. Red deer stalking, in the northern part of the island, provides an income for the estates, and at the same time helps maintain the ecological balance by essential culling. Culling occurs between August and February and if you intend to walk at this time make sure you use the **Hillphones service**, especially between August and late October, when stag stalking takes place. The hillphones service provides recorded messages detailing where stalkers are operating day-to-day

The Twelve Apostles, Catacol

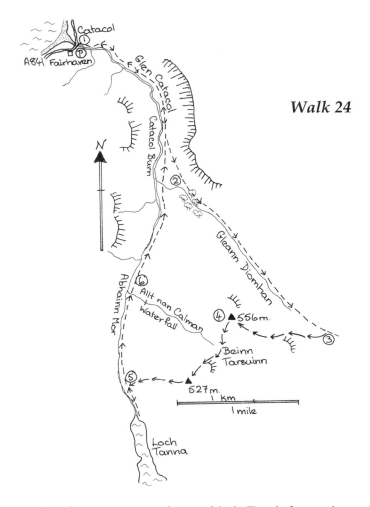

Walk 24

so that these areas can be avoided. For information tel 01770 302363.

The name **Beinn Tarsuinn** means *transverse hill*. There are at least three hills so named on Arran. This walk ascends the second in order of height. See walk 39 for the big one and walk 20 where you might spot a third (1151ft/352m) beyond Beinn Chaorach.

1 Cross the road and walk up the left side of the Catacol Burn for just over a mile to reach a cairn. Here the path divides and you take the left branch to begin a steady climb into Glen Diomhan, passing through heather. The way runs quite close to the edge of a steep-sided ravine through which the lively tributary burn finds its way to join the Catacol Burn.

2 Soon part of the ravine is fenced off by the Nature Conservancy, where a tall ladderstile gives access to the steep upper slopes of the gorge. Here two species of Whitebeam or Service tree are protected*. Continue climbing through the glen. Many streams descend in dramatic falls on either side of the burn and add their waters to the hurrying Diomhan. As the path rises to above 1,000ft/300m look for the low growing primitive club moss in the thin acid soil. Pause here and look back down the glen to the water of the Sound and to the shining surface of Lochan a'Mhill (walk 21) hidden in a hollow on Meall nan Damh.

3 Then the watershed of the burn is reached and the area is wet but there are plenty of convenient stones to help you across. From the ridge beyond, enjoy the superb view of Caisteal Abhail and Cir Mhor. On this extensive stony plateau cowberry and crowberry grow where they can. At the cairn, turn right off the ridge and climb up the gentle bilberry-covered slopes towards Beinn Tarsuinn and then along the shoulder to the summit cairn at 1819ft/556m. From here you can see ridge after ridge of the Southern Highlands.

4 Leave the cairn and walk on over the mile-long high stony plateau, with only a small dip in it, to Beinn Tarsuinn's lower

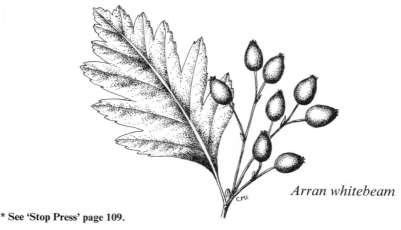

Arran whitebeam

* See 'Stop Press' page 109.

top, 1717ft/530m, keeping well away to the left to avoid the marshy watershed of the Calman waterfall. Then begin your descent down over the heather and juniper slopes, bearing steadily right (a little north of west). The descent seems to go on and on. As you go look for Dubh Loch and then Loch Tanna. Eventually you reach the path down through Glen Catacol. Here you may wish to turn left to walk on up the glen to Loch Tanna. It is the largest loch on the island and lies at 1100ft/340m. It is a sparkling sheet of water surrounded by the lower green slopes of the cradling mountains. Or you may wish to leave this for another walk and return from the foot of the path.

5 If so, turn right and begin your descent beside the wide, flat, smooth bed of the Catacol Burn, its banks lush with heather and ferns. Then you reach the spectacular Calman waterfall. It tumbles, hurtles and plummets from high on the slopes you have just walked. It drops over wide, chunky steps of granite in elegant cascades of white foam. Beside the fall, in a hollow that catches the summer sun, you might wish to picnic and paddle and explore the river gorge.

6 Then continue your descent, down the steepish path through a gorge. After crossing a barrier of glacial moraine over much of the valley bottom you cross the Diomhan Burn. Go on down the glen where you are soon joined by the path from Glen Diomhan, taken on your outward route. Continue on along the path to the parking area near the shore at Catacol Bay.

Practicals

Type of walk: Quiet and unfrequented high level walk, suitable for seasoned walkers.

Distance: 8 miles/13km
Time: 5 hours
Maps: OS Explorer 361/Landranger 69

NB All Arran's high granite peaks are in National Trust for Scotland's territory and so can be walked at any time of the year. But Beinn Bharrain isn't nor are these Catacol hills. Please use the hillphones service if appropriate.

25

The Postman's Path from Lochranza to Catacol and Lochranza Castle

Park in the public car park on the west side of Lochranza Pier, grid ref 925509. This lies on the right side of the road if driving along the A841from the village. It is opposite to the public toilets and a small cafe.

Lochranza Castle

Walk 25

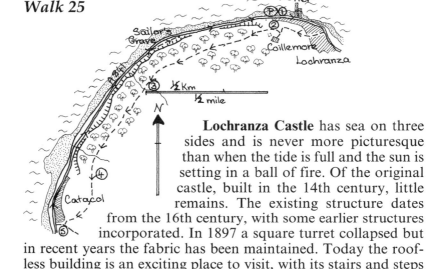

Lochranza Castle has sea on three sides and is never more picturesque than when the tide is full and the sun is setting in a ball of fire. Of the original castle, built in the 14th century, little remains. The existing structure dates from the 16th century, with some earlier structures incorporated. In 1897 a square turret collapsed but in recent years the fabric has been maintained. Today the roofless building is an exciting place to visit, with its stairs and steps to the various levels and the slits and other openings in the walls.

1 Walk back past the pier and cross the road and walk on until you reach the name sign for Claonaig Ferry. Here turn right along a track, signed 'Arran Coastal Path'. Go on to pass several houses and wind on with the track as it bears slightly right. Soon, turn off right at the Coastal Way marker, the access track continuing uphill to Colliemore, believed to be the oldest house on Arran. Follow the grassy track that takes you close to some of the buildings belonging to Colliemore. One is believed to have been a manse. Then go on past an old roofless house. Follow the pleasant grassy way and then bear right off it as directed by a Coastal Way marker. From here there is a fine view of Lochranza Castle and of Kintyre.

2 From now on the path can be very wet and deserves sometimes being called the 'wellie walk', but with good boots and taking care where you put your feet most people will manage this walk without getting their boots too wet. Walk on through young birch, where yellow topped posts lead you on along the narrow path. Then the way becomes drier as it passes through birch woodland. Go on through a clearing and then more birch woodland. As you go enjoy the magnificent view down to the Sound

far below. Keep following the yellow waymarkers: these are sometimes placed on stones, rocks, trunks of birch trees and telegraph poles. Continue, avoiding boggy patches, to arrive at another large clearing. Beyond, the path becomes much drier.

3 Cross a tiny burn with a step and then begin to descend over the open hillside on a waymarked path you share with deer. Then the path divides and it is marked with a yellow wooden 'flag'. Do not attempt to follow the lower path – a deer path. On the upper path you come, very shortly, to a yellow waymark and yellow blobs on the trees and you know that you are on the correct path. Go through more birch woodland, cross a stream and continue on a grassy way from where you can look down on the Twelve Apostles – see walk 23.

4 The path is grassy and still very high and from it are superb views. At the waymark, where the path divides, take the upper path to descend quite steeply. Soon you can see a large ladderstile onto a track, well below. Descend towards it by stepping across a stream and then following down the indistinct path. It moves across the slope, winds round a small hillock and continues to the last power line post. Then you need to curve right to walk beside the fence on your left to reach the large ladderstile, so avoiding a largish boggy area.

Common sandpiper

5 Once over, turn right and, at the road, turn right again to walk in front of the Twelve Apostles to start your return to Lochranza. The road runs along the shore and is rarely busy. Make full use of the good grassy verges, swathes of grass on the beach side, the beach, and then use a wide track under the very high cliffs, on the right, which cuts off a large stretch of the road. Finally a narrow grassy verge leads to the car park. Leave yourself time to explore the village, particularly the picturesque castle.

Roe deer

Practicals

Type of walk: This is a mainly level walk over cliffs. It is well waymarked but can be very wet in some parts. The views are superb. The return along the shore is a delight if you make full use of the beach, verges and the track that cuts off a corner.

Total distance: 4 miles/6.5km
Time: 2–3 hours
Maps: OS Explorer 391/Landranger 69

26

Newton, Fairy Dell

Drive to the end of the road at South Newton and park at the signposted layby, where stands a painted sign 'Trail to North Newton', grid ref 932514. This is reached by taking the side road, opposite Loch Ranza field centre. Cross the bridge over the Chalmadale burn and continue to the T-junction. Turn left and drive along the shore road to its end.

As you return along the shore look for **eiders**. You may hear the drake's delightful cooing call first, which he utters with head thrown up with a jerk, as if gulping. The drake is a handsome bird with white above except on the crown and lower back

Cottage, Fairy Dell

which, like most of the under parts, are black; the breast is a beautiful rose-buff. The duck is brown, mottled and barred with black. Both birds have bills sloping from the forehead. Eiders dive for molluscs on rocks or crustaceans in the weeds. Small molluscs are swallowed whole, but larger ones and crabs are crushed in the powerful bills; starfish and small cuttlefish are also eaten. They nest sometimes in heather or thrift in the open and often under the shelter of a wall or a rock.

1 Walk out of the back of the parking area on a grassy path between bracken. Then climb the narrow path as it winds a little left up the 'stranded cliffs'. At the top, go straight up the steepish sloping pasture until you need to wind left round the corner of the fenced garden of the The Whins, a craft shop. Continue past a picnic table to join a narrow reinforced track. Pause here for a magnificent view of the Claonaig ferry as it plies between Lochranza and Kintyre.

2 Turn left and walk the pleasing high level track, with gorse stretching up the hillside and an incredible view out over the Sound to the north end of Kintyre and Loch Fyne. At the division of the track, take the left branch and carry on from where you can see more of the Mainland. Where the reinforced track ends, go ahead as directed by the signpost along a grassy trod for half a mile towards the Fairy Dell, with the heathery slopes of Cnoc nan Sgrath to your right. Go on to where the way divides again. Ignore the muddy track that continues ahead and take the recently reinforced track that starts its steepish descent towards the Fairy Dell. The way

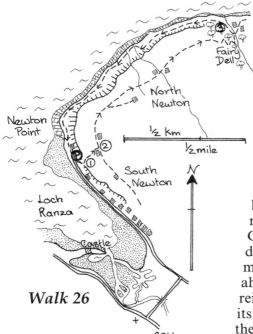

Walk 26

100

curves down the wooded slopes, where in spring primroses thrive, a cuckoo calls and the burn chatters on its way to the sea. At the foot of the track a white cottage and boat shed stand to your right.

3 Turn left and begin your walk along the Newton shore, the way at first wet and boggy and where you have to pick your way. At a 'suspect' stone circle, turn right as directed by a Coastal Way arrow, to walk towards the shore. Another arrow sends you left to continue just above the shoreline. This diversion avoids a very boggy area, taking you over boulders in places where it is rather wet. The path then leads you to a fine grassy and pebbly circle where, in the middle, stands a view finder – all part of the Coastal Way. Beyond, a footpath of fine granite, suitable for wheelchair users, returns you over what has always been a very boggy area to return to the parking area. Before you leave, stay awhile on the shore where you might see a common sandpiper, calling from the top of a boulder, alerting its mate and its young that people are about.

Eiders

Practicals

Type of walk: This is a glorious short walk, with fine views, mainly very good paths and with lots of bird life to be seen. Not to be missed.

Total distance:	2 miles/3.3km
Time:	1–2 hours
Maps:	OS Explorer 361/Landranger 69

27

South Newton, Laggan Cottage, An Scriodan, Newton Point

Park on the left, beyond The Lodge, South Newton, grid ref 938506. To access this, if approaching from the east (Brodick) on the A841, take a narrow road, turning off right just before passing Lochranza's church on the left. After a sharp left turn, pass the Lodge on the right, and park beyond on the left.

Lochranza

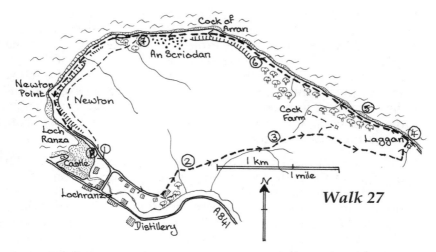

Walk 27

Cock Farm was the ancestral home of Daniel Macmillan, the book publisher, who was born there in 1813. He was an ancestor of Harold Macmillan who became Prime Minister.

The geologist **Dr James Hutton** went to Arran on a field trip in 1787 and discovered the island's remarkable variety of rocks. On this walk you will see his most important discovery, known as Hutton's Unconformity. An unconformity is produced in the following way: rocks are laid down usually under water on top of each other in a nice sequence. Then, much later, they are lifted up as mountains. They may be folded and tilted. Then they are eroded. They sink again and new deposits are laid on top. The place where the new and old rocks meet and the sequence is broken is the unconformity.

1 From the parking area, walk back along the narrow road, to reach a sharp bend. Here leave the road as it turns away right and head on along the continuing track, signposted to 'Laggan'. Pass several cottages and then, after ½ mile/1km, take the grassy left branch where the track drops down to more cottages at Narrachan. Follow the pleasing way as it climbs through bracken, where you might spot a merlin, flying low and silently, looking for prey. Cross the Eadaraidh Burn on a footbridge, where the hurrying water is shadowed by birches, willows and ferns. Go on climbing steadily, with splendid views to the right of the Sleeping Warrior (Caisteal Abhail) and the surrounding heights.

103

2 Continue climbing on the good path. This was once a very muddy section of the walk but it has, fairly recently, been reinforced by the Arran Access Project. As you near the top of the ridge, look right to see piles of slate waste. Slate is one of the oldest rocks on the island (600 million years) and was quarried in the 18th century by workmen who had to walk the hill every morning – the slates were used for roofing. Pause at the brow to enjoy the glorious view. The Sound of Bute lies below, with tiny boats appearing becalmed on its glassy surface.

3 The dry reinforced track then begins to descend steadily. To the right of the path steep craggy slopes rear up and on these a peregrine raises her brood. Away to the left steep, bracken-clad slopes run down to ruined crofts, including Cock Farm, where Harold Macmillan's ancestors lived. Continue along the wide grassy path, edged with white harebells. After a mile another ruined croft lies ahead, and just before this the path swings left and drops down and down to the shore beside Laggan Cottage (see walk 30).

4 Turn left by the cottage and follow the track along a raised beach through, in summer, bracken and a multitude of flowers. Close to the path the clear water of the Sound laps over pale grey sandstone boulders. Where an alder and birch wood lies ahead, take the rough path that runs just above the shore and below the trees. Beyond the wood are the remains of the old Laggan harbour. Look on the rocks, on the right, facing out to sea, for the famous fossil footprints of a giant centipede.

5 Continue a few steps along the path, to pass Duchess Anne's salt pan built in the early 18th century, and then coal shafts now filled with water. The coal from the thin seam was used to obtain the salt from sea water. Go through a gap in an old stone wall. Beyond, and up a slope, lies Ossian's cave. This is not a real cave but a hole among tumbled boulders, which has at some time provided shelter for fishermen and somewhere for them to store their nets and boxes.

6 Soon you pass through the dense shade of the towering cliffs of Torr Breac. The trees at the foot of the sheer rock face are alive with small songbirds. Then you reach a great rock fall. This is not the Fallen Rocks passed through on walk 30 but An Scriodan, where 270 years ago innumerable great boulders of sandstone tumbled from high above. There is a way through the boulders, which climbs quite high and requires some large steps up and down. The way only becomes difficult towards the end of the fall, but with care and some scrambling it is still passable. The best way is along the shore below the fall but at low tide only.

7 Wind on round the headland on the shore path below shallow cliffs. Go past a cottage (see walk 26), which is backed by fine woodland. At the next stream across your path, turn right to walk to the rocky shore. Here look for Hutton's Unconformity - red sandstone (laid down 400 million years ago) tilting towards the sea, overlying schist (thought to be about 600 million years old), providing evidence that the age of the earth was much greater than had been believed until that time. Stroll on along the good shore path to wind round Newton Point to return to where you have parked.

Merlin

Practicals

Type of walk: This is an exciting walk, with lots of spectacular views and with much of interest along the shore path.

Total distance: 9 miles/14.5km
Time: 5 hours
Maps: OS Explorer 361/Landranger 69

28

Gleann Easan Biorach and Gleann Diomhan Circular

Park close to Lochranza Castle, grid ref 932507. The village of Lochranza lies at the north end of the island and is reached by the A841.

The path through the top end of Glen Diomhan runs quite close to the edge of the steep-sided ravine through which the Diomhan burn finds it way, hurrying to join the Catacol burn. Soon you reach part of the ravine that has been fenced off by the Gleann Diomhan National Nature Reserve. A tall ladderstile gives access to the steep upper slopes of the gorge where both species of the whitebeam or service tree, ***Sorbus pseudo-fennicus*** and ***Sorbus Arranensis*** are protected from hungry deer. These trees are unique to Arran.

The Distillery, Lochranza

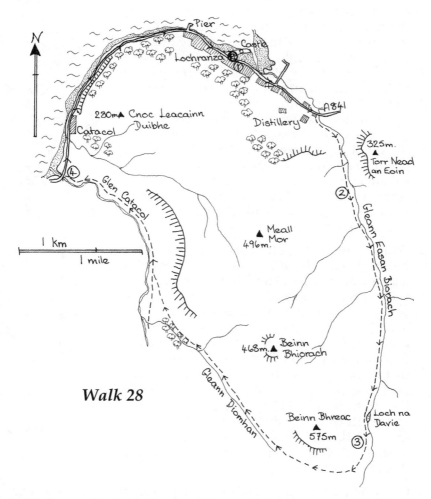

Walk 28

1 Walk south through the village of Lochranza enjoying the variety of buildings, the cottage gardens, and the ducks, swans and waders that make full use of the river before it reaches the sea. Look for the many wild flowers that adorn the roadside and then the fine distillery buildings on your right. Just beyond the latter, go past a cottage and turn right before the humpback bridge on the A-road along a grassy track, signed to 'Gleann Easan Biorach and Loch na Davie 3 miles'. The track runs along the riverbank under trees and is quite delightful. Soon it comes out into the open, goes past a small building (with a weir in the river on the left) and then narrows to a path. Climb the bank of the river terrace and follow the path along its edge, and up into the narrow cleft below Torr Nead an Eoin. In the depths below, you can hear a waterfall but cannot see it. Further on take a small diversionary path that descends steeply to give a view of a small waterfall and above it a low dam. Return up to the main path and continue on with a sturdy metal fence on your left along the top of the gorge. Where the fence stops go up a rather loose scree path and round a corner, and suddenly the glen opens out into a wide basin.

2   Walk on up the clear, though sometimes rather wet, path, enjoying the views of the mountains ahead and the sparkling burn full of more waterfalls to your left. In a little over a mile the valley closes in and the path begins to climb more steeply, although it becomes drier underfoot. Carry on uphill until you reach the diminutive Loch na Davie, on your left, and tucked under an outlier of the Castles. The loch lies on the watershed between Gleann Easan Biorach and Glen Iorsa, and most unusually its waters drain both ways. In summer look for the pale lilac-blue flowers of water lobelia swaying on long stems above the shallow water.

Water Lobelia

3   Carry on past a cairn and follow the path as it gradually swings right, round the west side of Beinn Bhreac. Follow the few small cairns to cross the high boggy col between Beinn Bhreac and Beinn Tarsuinn to come down into the head of Glean Diomhan, following a small rugged path on the eastern (right) side of the burn. Lower down, the rough path follows the right hand side of a deer fence, which keeps deer out of the Gleann Diomhan National Nature Reserve. At the end of the fencing take the higher path. This runs along the slopes below the crags but well above the Catacol Burn in the glen below. Then the path joins

the main path through the glen and after a mile comes to the bridge and the road at Catacol.

4 Turn right and walk on to pass the cottages known as the Twelve Apostles and the Catacol Bay Hotel. Continue on the road, which is rarely busy, making full use of the good grassy verges, swathes of grass on the beach side, the beach and then a wide track under very high cliffs on the right. The latter cuts off a longish stretch of the road. Finally a narrow grassy verge leads to the pier. Walk on to where you have parked at Lochranza Castle and if you were unable to manage a visit at the end of walk 25, perhaps you will be able to after this walk.

STOP PRESS

In November 2007 it was announced that a new species of tree had been discovered during research by Scottish Natural Heritage, Dougarie Estate and the Royal Botanic Gardens in Edinburgh. Two specimens of the tree had been found and they have been given the name Catacol whitebeam, *Sorbus pseudomeincichii*.

The tree is a cross between the native rowan and whitebeam. This new discovery brings the total number of tree species, unique to Arran, to three. To encourage seedlings to grow into mature trees the deer fence that currently surrounds the area is being extended to protect the trees from grazing deer.

Practicals

Type of walk: A quiet challenging walk into the hills beside a fine burn, past a small very interesting loch, and then descending through a wild glen where the Arran Service trees are protected. Expect plenty of wet walking after rain.

Distance:	10 miles/16km
Time:	5 hours
Maps:	OS Explorer 361/Landranger 69

29

The Castles

Park on the left of the road, just before the bridge over the North Sannox Burn, grid ref 993468. There is a sign 'Caisteal Abhail 4 miles'. To reach this take the A841 north to Sannox and then over the hill to North Glen Sannox.

Caisteal Abhail (The Castles) is the second highest mountain in Arran, 2753ft/847m. It gets its name from the huge granite tors that litter the summit. Its most famous feature is the spectacular gash formed by an eroded basalt dyke, known as the Witch's Step (Ceum na Caillich), on the ridge along the north side of Glen Sannox. Many walkers go this way; the Step can be by-passed without too much difficulty, but the path has become quite eroded. This walk takes a quieter route but one which gives fine views across to the Witch's Step.

The Castles (Caisteal Abhail) from the north

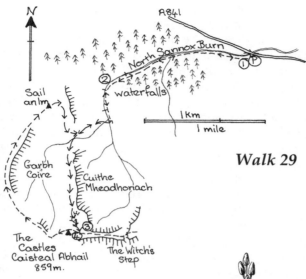

Walk 29

1 Leave the car park by the splendid path beside the North Sannox Burn. At first it is a 'wheelchair' path and there are seats beside it at intervals. Beyond the first burn it is not passable for wheelchairs but the surface continues to be good. Bell heather, cross-leaved heath and bog asphodel grow on the moor by the path. Go on through a gate in a deer fence into the forest and walk on beside the beautiful burn, which is all waterslides and crystal clear pools. Look for dippers and grey wagtails. The path winds through an open area by the burn, then through birch and rowan. The various side burns and drains that bisect the path are crossed by stepping stones, sometimes very large and far apart. There is a fine waterfall near the end of the forest path.

Bog asphodel and sphagnum

2 At the top of the forest, cross a ladder stile onto the open moor. This is the end of the made-up path, but a clear, though wetter, path continues beside the burn. Admire the narrow gorge where the entire water of the burn is constrained into a channel a few inches wide. The path runs along the edge of the river above the steep bank until it divides. Here you must cross; it is possible to climb down steeply below the confluence and cross, but it is easier to continue a few steps up the left tributary and then ford one burn at a time above the waterfalls. At the far side, work round to the right to join a clear small path from the lower crossing, which goes up the hillside towards the corrie lip above. The path becomes less distinct higher up and eventually disappears altogether, but continue heading for the ridge (Cuithe Mheadhonach) on the left (south) of the corrie lip. Cross the burn coming down from the Garbh Choire and climb the end of the ridge. The ground is quite steep but not difficult, with short grass and heather and gravelly steps. Look for deer below in the corrie; in June and July they may have calves, still with dappled coats. Soon the gradient eases but there are boulders everywhere; however any difficulties can be by-passed by finding small paths on the right (west) side of the ridge. Go on up long granite slabs, pleasing to walk up – when dry. Beyond these, keep right up a long grassy slope to a col, and then again to pass a fine granite tor on its right. The slope then steepens again; do not go too far to either side but keep to the crest of the ridge, until the way appears to be blocked with boulders. Here, follow a small path, right, and then climb an easy grassy path to reach the main ridge.

3 Here you join the obvious well-worn path along the ridge from the Witch's Step. Turn right, climb to another col, and then a steep scramble takes you onto the summit 'Castle'. This is a huge granite tor perched across the ridge. You feel really on top of the world. The views across Glen Sannox to Goatfell and Cir Mhor are superb, as are the views north up the Firth of Clyde.

4 Scramble back down to the col just below the summit (which you crossed on the way up) where a narrow exposed but otherwise straightforward path goes down on the left (north) side, by-passing the summit tors and returning you to the ridge to the west of them. The ridge here becomes wider, sloping down to the south-west, where there are more fine tors. Find the path which winds round to the right to follow the edge of the northern corrie,

Garbh Choire, and descend gently along the rim, over Carn Mor and then Creag Dhubh, neither of which require any more climbing. Bear gradually right to the top of Sail an Im. There is no definite path down from the latter and you have to work your way round to the right, heading south for the lip of the Garbh Choire. Wind round left again to descend to the North Sannox Burn to pick up the faint path you followed on the way up the hill. Ford the burn and its tributary at the confluence and return down North Glen Sannox on the excellent path to the car park.

Dipper

Practicals

Type of walk: A straightforward but little frequented way up a fine mountain. The views are superb. The scramble onto the summit tor could present a problem; if you don't like the look of it just miss it out. If you don't like the look of the path, which by-passes the summit, return by your ascent route. None of the mountains should be attempted in bad weather.

Total distance: 7 miles/11.4km
Time: 6–7 hours
Maps: OS Explorer 361/Landranger 69

30

North Sannox and the Fallen rocks

Park at North Sannox picnic site, grid ref 015466. This is well signposted, on the right, (east) if travelling north from Brodick on the A841.

The **North Sannox area** is rich in the remains of human habitation covering thousands of years. For example Bronze Age chambered cairns are to be found within the plantation. The picnic site at the start of the walk is close to Lag nan Sasunnach or the Hollow of the English, where Cromwell's soldiers, killed at Sannox, were supposedly buried. Nearer to present times, North Sannox and Laggantuine villages were cleared during the mid-19th century, to make room for deer and sheep, and their people moved to Canada. Within the forest are shielings used by the villagers for tending their cattle in summer.

The **'Measured Mile'** is marked on the land by tall posts and lights and used by ships for their speed trials.

The Fallen Rocks

The **Fallen Rocks**, to which this walk takes you, is a spectacular place where huge boulders have tumbled down the hillside. This major rock fall is believed to have occurred in the 1700s. The rocks are Devonian sandstone, a river deposit, believed to have been laid down 370 million years ago.

As you reach **Laggan** look for tiny pieces of coal about the path. This comes from a thin coal seam. Beyond the nearby trees is the site of the old harbour of the Laggan settlement where lived a farming community in the 18th century. A small industry flourished here, using the coal to produce salt from sea water.

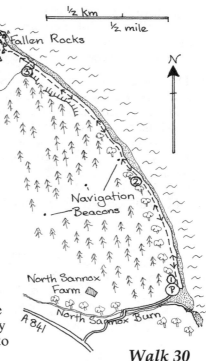

Walk 30

1 Leave by a deer gate at the end of the parking area. Carry on along the excellent track, with deer fencing to the right and, as you continue, birches clothing the shore beyond the fence. To the left the steep slopes are dark with lodgepole pine and hybrid larch, planted in the 1960s. Within the woodland there is evidence of raised beaches and former sea cliffs. Close to the path you can see several elderly oaks struggling to survive. These may be survivors of an area of oak planted in the 18th century.

2 Soon the good track comes close to the shore again, with large rugged fingers of rock stretching out into the sea. As you walk, look out to sea for mergansers, gannets, eiders and cormorants. You might also spot dolphins, or porpoises, or a basking shark. Here there are fine views across to the Firth of Clyde, to Great Cumbrae, Little Cumbrae and the Isle of Bute. Carry on past the Measured Mile post and follow the continuing track. Eventually the conifers are left behind and you can see the huge cliffs stretch-

115

ing up to your left, richly clad in vegetation. Here large boulders have fallen and have come to rest on the slopes. Today these are almost completely hidden under a dense layer of moss and opportunist flowers. Out of some boulders sprout crag-fast ash.

3 The track goes on, now grassy down the middle, and then when it ends, after 1¼ miles/2km, the way continues as a narrow path and climbs through a small outcrop of sandstone boulders. Go on along the shore where you might see otter footprints and then you come to a high ladderstile over a deer fence. Beyond are the Fallen Rocks, which you continue through on a twisty distinct path to the next set of Measured Mile beacons. Stroll on to turn round Millstone Point from where you can see Laggan cottage and stroll towards it and maybe beyond. Then retrace your outward route.

Gannet

Practicals

Type of walk: An easy level walk on a good track and then path. Return whenever you feel you have gone far enough.

Total distance:	3 miles/5km to the Fallen Rocks
	7 miles/11.3km to Laggan
Time:	1–2 hours/3 hour
Maps:	OS Explorer 361/Landranger 69

North Sannox Forest

Park at the Norh Sannox picnic site, grid ref 015466. To access this take the small side road which leaves the A841 about 1½ miles/1 km north of Sannox, signed to North Sannox.

Shielings were small huts used in summer when the animals were moved out onto the hill pastures. The people caring for the animals lived in the huts. There are several shielings in this wood although only one is by the path. They probably belonged to villages in North Glen Sannox, the remains of which can be seen across the burn from the road. The people were all evicted from here in 1829 to make room for a large sheep farm; they sailed to Canada where they settled in Megantic County.

There is a **pleasant grassy area** with seats across from the car park where you can look out to sea and watch gannets diving. Eiders and gulls frequent the mouth of the burn, as does a heron. Both sand and house martins fly low over the grass in summer, in pursuit of flies.

North Sannox Forest

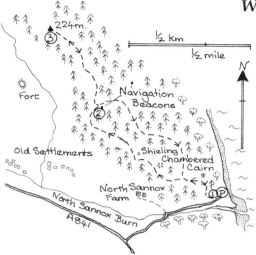

1 Go through the gate behind the car park into the forest and follow
the path as it curves up into the trees. At the Y-junction take the
waymarked left branch, which moves out into a more open area
with a picnic table and a fine view across to Glen Sannox. Follow
the path as it goes back into the trees. At a junction the right
branch is signed to a chambered cairn; it is not far off the path and
is worth a visit although not much remains. Continue on the path
to follow the next sign to the remnants of a shieling, again not far
off the path, just through a broken wall. Carry on along the path,
now no longer surfaced, as it climbs steeply up a wide ride.

2 At the top, the path swings left and then round to the right and
climbs to a Measured Mile post. A few yards on and you reach an
unmarked path junction. Take the left fork and wind round into
the trees again. For a short distance the path becomes indistinct
but soon improves and climbs up to a wide open area where the
waymarks reappear. Follow them across a slightly boggy, heathery
area, then up a slope with trees on the right. The walking here is
lovely with short grass and bilberry underfoot; and there are
superb views across to the left. At the top of the hill is a trig point
(739ft/224m) perched on a rocky knoll. If you climb the bank
across the path from the trig point and look down towards North
Glen Sannox you can see a fine iron age hill fort not far below you.

3 The path appears to continue but soon peters out in dense heather. Retrace your steps down through the open area to the unmarked junction by the Measured Mile post, and turn left. Descend the wide open ride, with views now out over the Firth of Clyde, and then turn down into the forest following a waymark. Go through a clearing and then into trees again, where at first the path is not obvious, but go straight ahead and it soon becomes distinct again. Wind on down, crossing the wall you saw on the way up, and eventually reaching the Y-junction where you turned left. Go on down the path to the gate and out to the car park.

Sand martin

Practicals

Type of walk: Easy and sheltered: just right for a windy day. Choose a day when the hills are clear because there are some fine views. The paths are mainly clear though not all surfaced and there are a few boggy areas.

Total distance: 2½ miles/4km
Time: 1–2 hours
Maps: OS Explorer 361/Landranger 69

32

Sannox to North Sannox

Park in the layby to the left of the large gates that give access to
the Sannox sand pit, grid ref 016455. To access this, leave
Brodick by the A841 and once through Corrie and Sannox look

*North
Sannox
Burn*

for the layby on the left side
of the road, just before the
fine bridge over the Sannox
burn. There is also a large
parking area, opposite the
signposted entrance to the
old mine road to Glen Sannox
but this is liable to flooding if
there are very high tides.

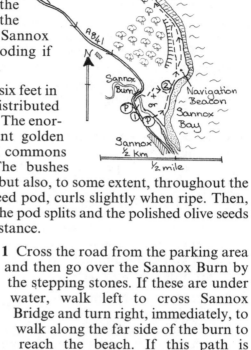

Walk 32

Gorse can grow up to six feet in
height. It is widely distributed
throughout the country. The enormous trusses of fragrant golden
flowers beautify heaths, commons
and seashore areas. The bushes
flower in early summer, but also, to some extent, throughout the
year. The black hairy seed pod, curls slightly when ripe. Then,
with a crackling sound, the pod splits and the polished olive seeds
are propelled to some distance.

*Manx
shearwaters*

1 Cross the road from the parking area
and then go over the Sannox Burn by
the stepping stones. If these are under
water, walk left to cross Sannox
Bridge and turn right, immediately, to
walk along the far side of the burn to
reach the beach. If this path is
flooded, walk on along the road
beyond the far end of the bridge
and turn right into a lane on
the right. Continue past
the old church on the
right and, soon after,
turn right to walk on
a short way to join
the path along the
shore, where you
turn left.

121

2 Enjoy the path just above the shore and then pass between gorse where there is a seat. From here, look out to sea where you might spot Manx shearwaters skimming or shearing the sea, rising and falling with the waves. At the Y-junction take the right fork and head towards a stand of birch. Then when you have another choice of paths, go ahead through trampled bracken towards more birch, avoiding a wet area. Very soon the path comes, on your left, below a huge much layered sandstone cliff, which supports many types of plants. Here you might spot people abseiling. Follow the path as it comes nearer to the shore once more before arriving at side of the North Sannox Burn, hurrying out to sea.

3 If the tide is out and there is little water coming down the burn, you might wish to cross it on a line of stepping stones, which are often wet and slippery. You may then wish to continue on along the coastal track to the Fallen Rocks and beyond (see walk 30). If the burn is impassable, continue on the good path upstream. This is a glorious way and if the river is in spate you have some most dramatic views. Continue to the bridge and cross it, right, and then walk downstream to the North Sannox picnic site and, if you wish, continue along the coastal path or complete the forest walk (see walk 31).

4 To return from North Sannox you may choose to retrace your outward route. Or you may prefer to ignore the bridge over the burn and go on up the continuing road to the A841. Here you turn left, making use of the little path that cuts off the corner, and then walk the ½ mile/1km back to the parking area.

Practicals

Type of walk: Short, easy and most pleasing.

Total distance by either route: 2 miles/3.5km. Add on extra miles if you continue along the route of walk 30 or 31 or both.

Time: 1 hour. Add on extra time if you continue along 30 or 31 or both.

Maps: OS Explorer 361/Landranger 69

33

Glen Sannox

Park as for walk 32, grid ref 016455.

In the cemetery, which you pass early on this walk, is the railed grave of **Edwin Rose**. In July 1889 Edwin, an Englishman, climbed Goatfell, with a Scotsman, John Laurie, whom he had met, a few days earlier, while walking on Bute. What happened on the mountain nobody is quite sure. Laurie came down alone, had a drink in a Corrie Bar and next day left Arran and drifted for two months between, Glasgow, Aberdeen and Liverpool before being apprehended for murder. Rose's decomposed body was eventually found high on the mountain, his skull shattered and his spine badly broken. At John Laurie's trial the jury had to decide whether he was pushed or did he slip. They decided that he was pushed and Laurie was sent to prison; he died 40 years later still in Perth Prison, at the age of 69, still protesting his innocence. Nowadays opinion is that Rose slipped and died and that Laurie took some of his possessions and hid his body.

Glen Sannox

Walk 33

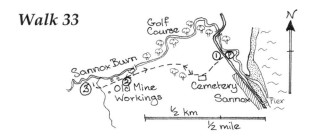

From 1840 onwards **baryte** was mined in Glen Sannox. But eventually the mine was closed by the 11th Duke of Hamilton because the buildings, waste heaps and other remnants spoiled the aspect of this glorious area. The mine was reopened after the 1914–18 war but the vein ran out just before the start of the 1939–45 war. Baryte, a white metallic element (barium sulphate), is used in some form or other in many industries including paint, paper, fireworks, matches and in the production of sugar.

1 Walk up the metalled road beyond the signpost. As you reach the cemetery you might like to go in and see the engraved stone on Edwin Rose's grave. Carry on up the continuing cart track and into the lovely glen, with large grassy open spaces and much bracken. Ahead are Suidhe Fhearghas, Ceum na Caillich, Cir Mhor and Cioch na h-Oighe. One moment their heads are in cloud, and the next their peaks float ethereally above brilliant white mist that moves and trails below the tops. Ignore the signed path to the footbridge and walk on beside a row of fine beech trees. Look here, on a low dead branch, for a spotted flycatcher, adroitly capturing flying insects. A short way along, take a narrow grassy way that bears off right and takes you to the few derelict buildings of the old baryte mine. Peep down, right, to see the scant remains of the water wheel. Carry on through another grassy hollow, where harebells grow, to see more remnants of the mine.

2 Then return to the main path and carry on where meadow pipits soar into the air and then descend trilling into the bog myrtle below. Soon you arrive at the side of the Allt a' Chapuill, a lively tributary burn of the Sannox Burn. From here look across right and up the slopes to see fenced-off mine shafts and their tips of waste. Cross the burn on convenient boulders and carry on up

124

beside the main burn. If you wish to continue into the glen, the best way lies on the opposite bank and you will have to choose a good crossing place – in spate this will be difficult. Alternatively return to the bridge and continue up the path on the far bank from there. This easy-to-tread path takes the walker deep into the glen and to the point from which to commence the climb to The Saddle between Glen Sannox and Glen Rosa (walk 34).

3 Return by your outward route.

Spotted flycatcher

Practicals

Type of walk: A lovely, short or longer walk that can be enjoyed by all

Total distance: 2 miles/3.4km or more
Time: 1–2 hours
Maps: OS Explorer 361/Landranger 69

34

Glen Sannox and Glen Rosa via the Saddle

As this is a linear walk you may wish to make use of Arran's good bus service from Brodick to just before Sannox Bridge (obtain leaflet from TIC, Brodick pier). If walking this long route with friends, park one car as for walk 32 and the second as for walk 39.

The *Arran mountains* have been shaped by glaciers. Both Glen Sannox and Glen Rosa are typical U-shaped valleys, and the hills have been cut back until they form narrow ridges or aretes. There are high corries up above the main glens; the one you see well on this walk is Coire nan Uaimh (sometimes called the Dress Circle) between Cir Mhor and the Castles. Below it are ice-polished slabs of granite. The Saddle that divides Glen Sannox from Glen Rosa slopes gently down on the Glen Rosa side but has been cut back by the glacier into a steep cliff on the Glen Sannox side, the Whin Dyke forming the only sensible means of ascent for walkers.

The Castles from the Saddle

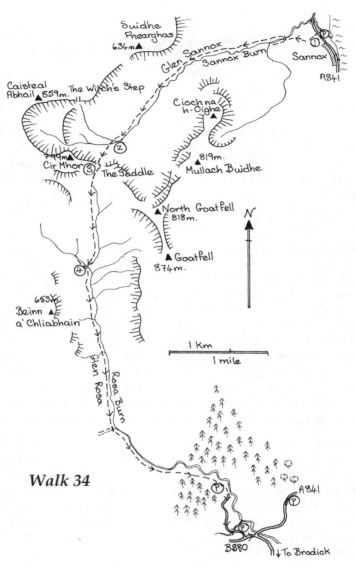

Walk 34

1 Walk the track up Glen Sannox as already written in walk 33. At
the fine stand of beech, turn right and cross the good bridge over
the Sannox Burn. Turn left at the far side and follow a somewhat
rough path up the side of the burn and on into the glen. A little
further up the glen the path has been improved and is now well-

Kestrel

drained and surfaced, so walking it is much easier. Enjoy the views of Cioch na h-Oighe to the left and Suidhe Fhearghas to the right, but it is the lovely symmetrical cone of Cir Mhor, in the centre, which dominates the scene. As you continue the Witch's Step comes into view on the right, with the Castles (Caisteal Abhail) behind. To the left of Cir Mhor is a low col: this is the Saddle, and your way goes over it.

2 Near the head of the glen cross the Sannox Burn on good stepping stones, and begin the climb to the Saddle. The path turns right into the Whin Dyke. This is a basalt dyke intruded into the granite that has weathered out to leave a groove, giving a relatively straightforward route up the steep headwall of the glen. There is a looser rocky scrambly bit up the lower part of the Whin Dyke. Above the loose path (easier to go up than to come down) there is a section of easy scrambling on good firm rock, followed by a pitched staircase. This replaces the path that had become very eroded in the top part of the gully, and the improvement makes this a much more enjoyable walk. At the top of the steps the path heads off to the left to the crest of the Saddle.

3 The top of the Saddle is a wonderful place to eat your lunch. Select a comfortable seat among the enormous granite boulders and enjoy the spectacular scenery, knowing that the most difficult part of the walk is now behind you. Ravens float around the crags, enjoying the thermals, and kestrels hover in the updraught. Find the distinct path, which leads down into Glen Rosa. This side slopes very gently, and the path has been well made although there are some rough bits near the top.

4 Cross the Rosa Burn on rather awkward stepping stones and walk down beside it. Like all the Arran burns the water is clear, without peat, and the granite pebbles look golden. There are deep pools for a swim, and waterfalls, and places where the water slides over granite boiler plates. Stop from time to time to look

back at the lovely view. Go through an enclosure to exclude deer, using high kissing gates, and then cross the bridge over the Garbh Allt. The path becomes a track and turns round the corner so the view of Cir Mhor which has been with you all day is now gone. Head on to cross a wide stile beside a gate and climb up a slope, then the track becomes a metalled road. Follow it to your second car, or out to the String Road, where you turn left, then right at the junction, to walk carefully into Brodick. Or you may pick up a convenient bus but it is almost as quick to walk.

Raven

<hr />

Practicals

Type of walk: Some walkers consider it to be the best in Arran and among the best in Scotland. It is quite long and not to be attempted lightly as it takes you into the heart of the hills. The ascent of the Saddle involves some scrambling which is not difficult but may deter some people; be prepared to turn back if you find it is not for you or if the weather changes.

Total distance:	10 miles/16km
Time:	6–7 hours
Maps:	OS Explorer 361/Landranger 69

35

Coire na Ciche

Park in the large car park, grid ref 016454, on the east side of the A841 just before the bridge over the Sannox Burn. If very high tides are expected park on the other side of the road in a large space to the side of the entrance to the Sannox sand pit. (see walks 32 and 33)

Cioch na h-Oighe, the maiden's breast, is a dramatic, steep, but not particularly high mountain (2148ft/661m) enclosing Glen Sannox on its south side. Its spectacular corrie, **Coire na Ciche**, translates as the Corrie of the Breast but is more generally known as the Devil's Punchbowl and when you see it with the mist swirling up around the cliffs it is easy to imagine him cooking up some noxious brew. The corrie is a place where you can enjoy the seclusion and drama of the mountains without too much climbing.

Ciche na h-Oighe and the Devil's Punchbowl

1 From where you have parked take the nearby track signed, 'Glen Sannox'. Walk on past the cemetery to go through a gate. Follow the track up the glen past a fine stand of beech trees and then through old mine workings to come to a burn, the Allt a'Chapuill. Do **not** cross this but turn left on a narrow path, which runs up beside it. The path is good and continuous, but in summer runs through head-high bracken in places so take care as you negotiate the hidden rocks and steps in the path. Go past a small empty dam and then notice an open mine shaft on the left; it is very deep and unprotected so take care. The burn on the right flows through a gorge, but where you have glimpses of it is most attractive.

2 Further on, turn right on an open obvious path to ford the burn which is no longer in its gorge. Almost immediately the path forks; take the left branch which leads across a rather boggy flat to the Allt a'Chapuill again, and continues up its bank. Here it is much drier underfoot, with thyme and harebells in summer. You may be lucky enough to see a hen harrier hunting over the moor. There are birch and rowan trees beside the burn, which plunges down in a series of waterfalls as the way gets steeper. Carry on up the mostly dry path as it climbs steadily to the lip of the corrie. High up the path becomes intermittent and you will have to pick your way round bogs and boulders, using the many animal tracks.

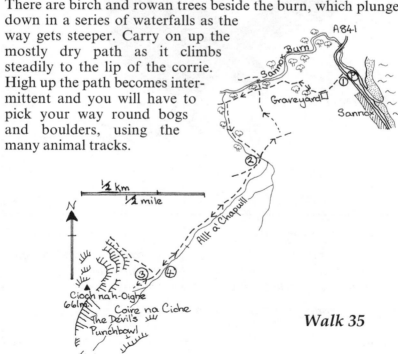

Walk 35

3 Go up into the remote, secluded corrie. Eventually the faint path crosses the burn and you may wish to stop here. The rock scenery is magnificent, with great seamed cliffs on the north side and the pinnacled ridge of Cioch na h'Oighe soaring above. The views out of the corrie over the Firth of Clyde to the mainland hills are also fine. You may hear ring ouzels and might see a kestrel.

4 Retrace your steps down by the waterfalls until you reach the ford over the Allt a'Chapuill again. Go straight ahead here on a clear track, which contours below a small hill and then begins to disappear. Look downhill and you will see an obvious quad bike track leading towards the stand of beech trees passed at the start of the walk. Go down this to rejoin the main track up the glen, where you turn right to return to the car park.

Ring ouzel

Practicals

Type of walk: This is an easy but quite strenuous walk on clear but unsurfaced paths, except for the final slope up into the corrie where you have to make your own way. Avoid in mist.

Total distance:	4 miles/6.5km
Time:	2–3 hours
Maps:	OS Explorer 361/Landranger 69

36

Goatfell

Park close to the start of the signposted route from Corrie to Goatfell, grid ref 026422. There is also ample parking, either on the shore opposite the sign, or in a layby further towards Corrie village itself. Corrie lies north of Brodick on the A841.

Goatfell, Arran's highest mountain (2866ft/874m), is very popular with visitors but walkers should remember that it is a mountain and all the appropriate precautions for high-level walking apply.

On the high slopes you might see **ptarmigan**. These birds only occur on the highest mountains of Scotland and some of the western islands. It is a bird of rocky summits, where lichens and mosses replace more luxuriant vegetation. They seldom breed below the 2,000ft contour. They are white in winter. In spring they go patchy and in summer they look like grey speckledy hens. They are more invisible in summer really, unless they move. They have white wing feathers so are always visible when flying.

View from the top of Goatfell

Walk 36

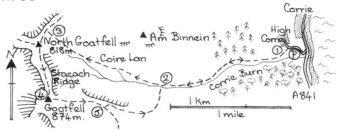

1 From the signpost, follow the track striking uphill, with the Corrie Burn, away to your left and a deer fence to your right. The burn is often known as White Water because of its many white-topped waterfalls. Go on ascending the well pitched steep way, with the magnificent burn now closer to you. Go through a deer gate and continue on up.

2 Eventually the slope eases and you should carry on to where the path divides. Ignore the fine pitched way, leading off left to cross the burn, and go on bearing half right along less steep ground. After this more 'restful' quarter of a mile, comes a very steep climb to the cairned ridge ahead, where sheer granite walls, with a multitude of fractures, rear upwards on either side of the path. At the cairn, pause to look over the ridge into Glen Sannox and the steep crags beyond.

3 Turn left and walk on over the summit of North Goatfell (2666ft/820m) and then descend a little to continue in the direction of Goatfell, along the Stacach ridge. There are two routes you can take towards the highest mountain. The lower rough path, on your left, leads on with few problems, across the mountainside. The upper path, the Stacach route involves climbing through a small 'chimney', clambering down some steep rock steps, walking along a flattish area and climbing a 'passage', before starting down more rock steps. None of this is very difficult; the granite is rough and firm and the safe route through these obstacles is fairly easy to find, though care is needed. Don't stray too far right where the way becomes exposed.

4 At the end of the Stacach the two paths converge and continue to the summit of Goatfell and its solid cairn. On a clear day, the views are marvellous in all directions. Close to are the surround-

ing Arran peaks, with glimpses of Loch Tanna and Loch na Davie. Beyond, to the west, lies Kintyre with a sparkling sea on either side of the peninsula. Further north-west lie the mountains of Jura and then Mull, with the highland peaks just discernible. To the north-east the Cumbraes and the Isle of Bute float like toys on blue water. To the south Ailsa Craig rears up out of the sea with Holy Isle to its west. To the west a faint darkening on the horizon is Ireland. Then begin your descent. Look for the mainly pitched way descending, east.

Ptarmigan

5 At a cairn the path divides. To return to Corrie, take the continuing stepped path on the left. (The right branch continues on down the much improved track to Brodick Castle where the early parts of the path were used in walk 37a; but you then have the problem of how to return to your vehicle at Corrie). Follow the long stone staircase down and down to arrive at the Corrie Burn, ignored on the way up, which you cross on large boulders and which will only present problems after very heavy rain. Then return down by your outward path.

Practicals

Type of walk: A mountain walk that will suit seasoned walkers. Once the path used on your descent was a quagmire for part of the way, now after excellent work by the Arran Access Group the route is in no doubt.

Total distance:	8 miles/13km
Time:	5–6 hours
Maps:	OS Explorer 361/Landranger 69

37a

A walk through the grounds of Brodick Castle

Waterfalls, Merkland Burn

Park in the car park at Brodick Castle, grid ref 018378. The castle lies 2½ miles/4km north of Brodick pier and is signposted off the A841.

As the ferry approaches the pier everyone looks with delighted surprise at the lovely bay of Brodick and at the dramatic mountains cradling the picturesque **red sandstone castle**, set among fine trees. The apartments in the castle were used by the Duchess of Montrose, the last member of the Hamilton family to do so. She ensured that the castle was well endowed when she gave it into the care of the National Trust for Scotland, in lieu of death duties. The public were given access to the gardens and many small paths were added.

Much work has been done on the **paths** used on

Walk 37a

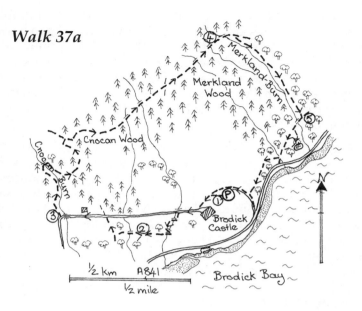

this walk and, near the end of point 2, a notice board says 'The continued pressures of erosion from walkers and the high rainfall often leave the paths waterlogged or deeply scarred. All the (repair) work is being done sensitively by Scottish Natural Heritage, Scottish Mountaineering Trust, Regional Development Trust and the Highland and Islands Development Trust.' Their work is much appreciated.

Rhododendron ponticum was introduced in the 1800s when the gardens of the castle were landscaped. These bushes, now considered weeds, have smothered many parts of the estate. Recent efforts by hundred of volunteers and contractors have removed many acres, allowing beech, birch, oak and alder to flourish once more. This is seen clearly in Merkland Wood, which is 400 years old and once was a source of timber for the island.

1 From the car park, walk over to the right side of the shop and wind on round to its entrance. Then stroll uphill on a tarmacked drive. Cross the entrance road to the castle, which lies to your left. Continue on the reinforced path through deciduous woodland and turn left to walk along a road, passing the castle on your left. Opposite a gate that says 'danger deep water', turn left

137

into a path and then, almost immediately, bear right and follow the railed way. Look back to see the burn descending in a white-topped waterfall as it passes under the road. Continue on the delectable path beside the lovely stream. Go on past a seat and then cross a footbridge to walk under huge Noble firs. Follow the twisty path to join a wider path, where you turn right to descend. Go over the bridge across the lovely Mill Burn and carry on to a junction of paths.

2 Here take the immediate right, the upper path, and walk ahead to join the Goatfell path, ignoring the Easceanoch Trail beyond the gate on the left. Carry on along the track, with great banks of rhododendrons on either side and then, when passing sheep pastures, you have an excellent view of BenNuis. At the next junction turn left onto a road, leaving the Goatfell footpath to pass, on your right, the old kennels (private dwellings). Cross an easy-to-miss bridge over a braided part of the Cnocan Burn and then in a step or two you reach the main bridge over the burn, where you might like to peer over, with care, into the steep sided ravine, through which the burn flows.

3 At the end of this bridge, turn right to walk a path high along the side of the lovely Cnocan Burn. Then take a signed path descending right to the Duchess's bathing pool. This is a deep, cold double pool, constantly kept moving by a tiny fall above and is a pleasing corner in which to take a pause. Return up the path and turn right to walk on to cross a sturdy bridge. Carry on along the main path with a wonderful view downstream. At a junction of paths, turn left and walk in the direction of the signposted Goatfell Track. Then go left at the Track and carry on following the red waymarks. Pass under many Western Hemlock trees, their branches laden with tiny cones. Wind round right, with the track, ignoring all other routes, still following the red arrows, to walk a rising wide ride. At the next junction leave the Goatfell Track and go sharply right on the red way-marked path. Here conifers meet overhead.

Western hemlock

4 Descend a little to cross the Merkland Burn on a footbridge. Just beyond, take an easy-to-miss right turn, onto an open space, with a picnic table. Then go on down the now clear path, with the cascading burn to your right. To the left stand scattered oaks from where rhododendrons have been removed. Continue on down past a fine stand of beech also now free of the same weed. Across the burn the sheer side of the gorge is almost completely hidden by the rampaging rhodies. Follow the twisting path down and down until you turn right on a track, where you re-cross the lovely burn.

5 Walk down the wide track until you can turn left to curve round on a little path, which brings you to the Heronry Pond. After a pause here, continue right to return to the main track and walk on down. Bear right just before you reach the A841 and walk towards a gate into pasture land. Do not pass through but turn left into woodland and follow a little path. Here many rhododendrons have been cleared. At the entrance road to the castle, turn right and a few steps along, look for the fascinating cork oak, on your left, and then continue uphill to the car park.

Wren

Practicals

Type of walk: A real must. The paths and tracks are good and the beauty of the estate is spellbinding.

Total distance:	4 miles/6.5km
Time:	2–3 hours
Maps:	OS Explorer 361/Landranger 69

37b

Brodick Standing Stones

Park in the car park on right side of the road at Cladach, grid ref 012376. To reach this, take the A841 north from Brodick for just under a mile.

When completing this walk the writer continued along the road, towards Corrie, where it comes close to the shore. Here a protective wall has drainage holes spaced regularly along its base. One of these gave shelter to a **nightjar**. It crouched, exquisitely

Standing Stones, Brodick

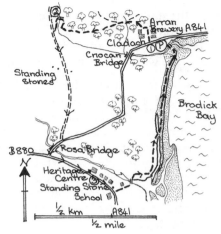

Walk 37b

camouflaged, against dead grass and the warm coloured stone-work. Walkers, joggers, cyclists and motorists passed by not noticing its rounded head, long tail, sparkling eyes and short beak. During the day the nightjar lies silent upon the ground, often on a heap of stones looking like a bit of lichen-covered twig or a piece of bark. It flies at dusk, often at sundown, a long-tailed shadowy form with easy, silent moth-like flight. This relatively rare and elusive bird is known to nest in the woodlands around Brodick Castle, probably its most northerly location in Britain. The woodlands, a mixture of tall trees, thicket and open spaces with song perches, provide just the habitat for the nightjar to thrive.

1 Cross the road from the car park and take the track opposite, signed 'Goatfell Path', which also goes to the Arran Brewery. Walk up between the buildings and wind round to the left and then right. Go uphill a short way and follow the path as it bends left again and levels out. It is a lovely path through fine trees.

Nightjar

141

Cross a burn by the bridge and at a bend, where the path begins to climb again, go through a gate, on the left, signed Easceanoch Trail. Go down the path, which runs along through the lower edge of the woods. Eventually it turns right and leads to a bridge over the Cnocan Burn, which you cross, and then turn left.

2 Follow the path until it meets the exit drive from the castle. Turn left and stroll down the road, which is lined on both sides by magnificent beech hedges. Peer through gaps to see two standing stones in the field on your right and then one in the pasture to your left. Walk on down the drive to the entrance gates, pass through and turn right along the A-road. Cross the Rosa Burn on a humped bridge and go left with the road. Use the verges where possible and take care as the road can be busy. Go past Arran Heritage Centre (open April to October), which you might like to visit, including its café.

3 Ignore the signed footpath just beyond it and walk on to pass the school on the right and a huge standing stone in the hedge on your left. Just past this, take a path on the left, by a small parking place, and walk down to the golf course. Cross the bridge over the Rosa Burn and turn right along the far bank. Wind left behind the shore, up a shallow valley with the golf course to your left and with the beach beyond a low line of dunes, to your right. You may prefer to cross over the dunes to walk on the shore as soon as the wet patch to your right runs out. The view across the wide sweep of Brodick Bay to the castle and its woodlands is superb. As you walk along the beach, look out for seals, cormorants and curlews until you reach a river, the Cnocan Burn. Turn inland a little, cross a footbridge, then follow the path at the far side, which in a very short distance brings you back to the car park.

Practicals

Type of walk: Pleasant easy stroll

Total distance: 2 miles/3.2km
Time: 1 hour
Maps: OS Explorer 361/Landranger 96

A low-level walk through Glen Rosa

Parking is always difficult for a walk through Glen Rosa. There is space for about three cars on the right just before Glenshurig Bridge, down the Glen Rosa road, grid ref 002369. There is also a reasonably sized car park by the cemetery where the Glen Rosa road turns off the String Road. Apart from this there are occasional spaces along the road if you tuck yourself well in,

Pool, Glen Rosa

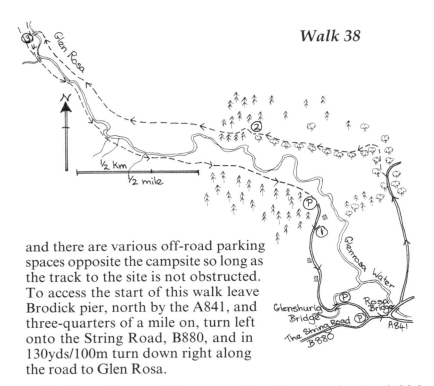

and there are various off-road parking spaces opposite the campsite so long as the track to the site is not obstructed. To access the start of this walk leave Brodick pier, north by the A841, and three-quarters of a mile on, turn left onto the String Road, B880, and in 130yds/100m turn down right along the road to Glen Rosa.

On this walk you might see an **adder**. They are short and thick in body in contrast to the grass snake and the smooth snake, which both have gracefully tapered bodies. The adder has a short tail. The iris of the eye is coppery-red and the pupil is a vertical ellipse. This usually means they are active at night but the adder is also active by day. Body colouring is variable but their most

Adder

characteristic mark is the dark zig-zag line down the centre of the back, with a series of spots on either side. They are usually found in dry places, for example, sunny slopes of hills or hedge banks. They feed on lizards, mice, shrews, voles, young weasels, birds, frogs, newts and large slugs. Accidents to humans from their bites are very, very rare and they are much more afraid of you than you are of them. But of course you should keep an eye open and if you do spot one, stand still and let it hurry away.

Grass of Parnassus

1 Walk back along the Glen Rosa road to the junction with the String Road and turn left, then left again onto the main road. Cross the bridge over the Rosa Burn and turn left in through the gates to the grounds of Brodick Castle. Walk up the exit driveway, peeping through gaps in the high beech hedges for a glimpse of the standing stones (see walk 37b). Then follow the road uphill and take a track on the left, just before a bend, signed 'Rosa Bridge' and follow it as it climbs below fine oak and beech trees. Go with the track as it turns sharply left and is signed 'Rosa Loop' and dawdle downhill, with a row of mature sycamores on the left and clear-fell that is beginning to regenerate on the right. In summer you might see speckled wood butterflies along here.

2 Go through a gap in an old wall and wind left, soon to enter a dark conifer plantation where the path is not clear. Keep on just inside the trees at the lower edge of the plantation to reach a gate in a deer fence, where you emerge onto the open fell. The path is now very distinct and runs along the edge of the river terrace through bracken or sometimes as a broad grassy swathe. There are a few wet places but these can be by-passed. Finally the path becomes stony and crosses the steeper hillside to round the corner in the glen. In summer the grass is bright with thyme,

145

harebells and lady's bedstraw. Occasionally, if you are lucky, you may catch a glimpse of an adder slithering off the path. Descend to a fine wooden footbridge across the Rosa Burn. There is a deep pool below where people jump off the bridge into it. If you spend some time looking into the pool you can see brown trout, some of which are quite large. This is a lovely place to have lunch. Alternatively you can turn right along the far bank of the burn and walk upstream to another superb pool with granite boiler plates below it and a wonderful view up the glen to Cir Mhor.

3   From either pool, follow one of several paths across the grass to join the main path down Glen Rosa. Turn left, soon to cross the bridge over the Garbh Allt and carry on down the glen. The path becomes a wide sandy, pebbly track along the floodplain of the Rosa Burn. Cross a wide stile beside a gate and walk along the continuing reinforced track uphill to the campsite, then follow it (now metalled) back to your car.

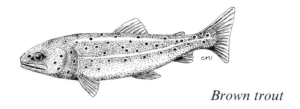

Brown trout

Practicals

Type of walk: A pleasant fairly short round which takes you into Glen Rosa and allows you to enjoy the spectacular views and the lovely burn without the long walk up into the hills. The paths are mostly good, with just a few wet places, and although there is some road walking it is mainly on narrow quiet roads. The only difficulty, as with all walks in Glen Rosa, is parking.

Total distance:	5 miles/8km
Time:	2 hours
Maps:	OS Explorer 361/Landranger 69

39

The Three Beinns

Drive the single track road, off The String, to where the tarmac ends, opposite Glen Rosa's camping site, grid ref 002376. There are various off-road parking spaces here, so long as the track to the site is not obstructed. Some walkers take the chance of continuing down the track to the first locked gate. But here there is only off-road space for two or three cars, and if these are all occupied the driver faces the problem of turning in a confined space and going back to the area first described. To access this, approach north from Brodick pier on the A841, and after ¾ mile/1.3km turn right onto The String road just before you cross

The Old Man of Tarsuinn

the Rosa Bridge. Then in 130yds/100m turn right into the narrow road, signed Glen Rosa.

The three beinns, **Beinn Nuis** (2597ft/792m), **Beinn Tarsuinn** (2706ft/826m) and **Beinn a'Chliabhain** (2141ft/675m) are all over 2000ft/600m. These are granite mountains and are great for scrambling. Beinn Nuis is sadly famed for three wartime plane crashes that claimed 20 young lives. Beinn Tarsuinn has its 'Old Man', a rock formation that lies to the right of the path. Beinn a'Chliabhain's west face drops almost sheer to glorious Glen Rosa far below.

1 From the end of the narrow road, walk along the continuing track above the Rosa Burn. Climb the stile beside a gate and then go through a kissing gate. Carry on until after 1½ miles/2.5km you can cross the sturdy footbridge over the Garbh Allt, which slides, tumbles and flows exuberantly over its rocky tree-lined bed.

2 Beyond, turn left and begin the fairly arduous uphill climb beside the impetuous burn to reach a kissing gate into a fenced area, the fence in place to allow tree regeneration round the burn. Here the path has been improved. Leave the enclosure by another gate and go on up. Eventually the path does become more level. Walk on

Walk 39

until you can pass through a second, large enclosure, and here the burn makes a big right-hand bend. Continue upstream until you can see a cairn on the opposite bank and cross by some boulder hopping. If the burn is in spate this may need wading or paddling (or returning). Once across, turn right and continue for a quarter of a mile, along the side of the burn. Then follow the path as it swings left to the foot of a steep rocky ridge and go with it as it ascends the rib on a distinct path for about a mile to the summit Beinn Nuis. As you go enjoy the magnificent views of Iorsa Water, Loch Tanna and Beinn Bharrain, and across Kilbrannan Sound to the Mull of Kintyre.

3 Pause at the top for dramatic views of Goatfell and North Goatfell – and perhaps lunch. Continue along the clear path towards the summit of Beinn Tarsuinn. Stroll the gently climbing way, watching out, on the right, for the Old Man, a gigantic weather-sculpted 'head'. A few minutes after this you reach the flat top of Beinn Tarsuinn, with its small cairn on top of a huge boulder, to the right of the track.

4 Then begin the descent from Tarsuinn, keeping well left where the path is indistinct. This is particularly so after passing a small cave where keeping ahead leads to a long flat sloping rock and a sheer drop. The real route turns sharp left before the rock is reached. Near the bottom of the track a little rock scrambling is required. Here, again, keep left of some sloping slabs. Follow the path as it swings right of a high pinnacle; it is essential to turn right here and continue south-eastwards towards the summit of Beinn a'Chliabhain. The reason is because the route, if you go ahead (north) by mistake, leads over erratically-spaced boiler plates on to the A'Chir ridge, which are dramatic to behold, but are likely to severely frighten all but the most experienced and level-headed scramblers. Therefore after taking the right fork continue along a narrow rocky ridge and up a grassy slope. Go on steadily climbing along the distinct path to the rocky summit of Beinn a'Chliabhain. The path then leads out of a huge granite boulder chaos onto a grassy platform for an extensive view over Brodick. Here you might see a golden eagle, ascending in slow circles until out of sight.

5 Now begin the descent over an easy-to-follow path. Where it seems to branch, keep to the right fork and gently descend the

long ridge to the cairn on Cnoc Breac (1330ft/409m). Continue downhill until you reach the moorland plateau. Very shortly the path takes you through peaty moorland and your wonderfully dry high-level walk is over. Continue on until you reach the side of the Garbh Allt.

6 Turn left and begin the descent, passing through the lower enclosure. It seems even harder work than the ascent, but this time you have the satisfaction of thinking about what you have already achieved to keep you going until you reach the valley bottom. Turn right and cross the footbridge. Retrace your outward route along the track to the parking area.

Golden eagle

Practicals

Type of walk: This is a fine route over a horseshoe-shaped ridge. The first climb and the last descent over steep moorland are arduous, but once you are up it is glorious. Suitable for seasoned walkers.

Total distance:	9–10 miles/14.5–16km
Time:	6–7 hours
Maps:	OS Explorer 361/Landranger 69

Cir Mhor

Park as for walk 39

Cir Mhor (the Great Comb) is a Corbett. It is 2600ft/799m and therefore not high enough to be a Munro, which is the name given to mountains over 3000ft/914.4m. It is one of the most spectacular of the Arran hills. Its position at the head of both Glen Sannox and Glen Rosa and its beautiful symmetrical shape ensure that it dominates the view up both glens.

Stags cast their antlers every spring and then regrow them. The new antlers are covered in furry skin, called velvet, until they are fully grown when the skin dies and the stag rubs it off. He then has a fine new set of antlers ready for the rut (mating season) which is in September and October.

1 Leave your parking area and walk on to the turning space and over the wide stile by the gate. Continue on the sandy, gravelly

Cir Mhor

path, which runs along the flood plain of the Rosa Burn. After a mile the glen bends round to the north and you can see Beinn Chliabhain and then the serrated ridge of A'Chir. Finally the dramatic cone of Cir Mhor, the walk's objective, appears, and from now on it dominates the view. Cross the sturdy wooden bridge over the Garbh Allt and carry on up the glen for another two miles. Much work has been done on the path and it is now mostly well drained and firm. Enjoy the unfolding views of the mountains, and the delightful Rosa Burn, which runs near the path in a series of waterfalls and slides over granite boiler plates. Look for deer; in summer you may see stags with their antlers still in velvet. Go through a kissing gate into an area fenced against the deer to allow tree regeneration to take place, then through a gate out of it. Carry on until you reach the crossing of the Rosa Burn.

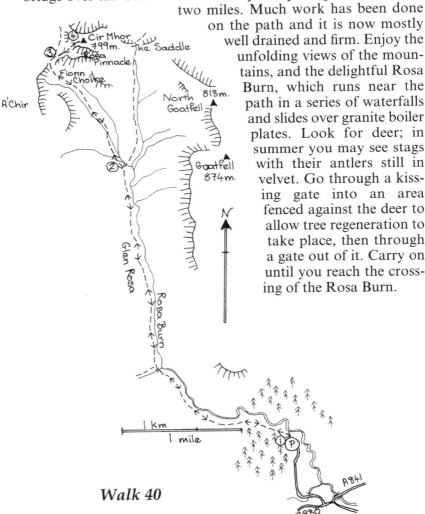

Walk 40

152

Red deer stag in velvet

2 Do **not** cross but follow an indistinct path along the river bank. It is boggy at first but soon improves. Cross two small side burns on good stepping stones, and then go over the main burn flowing out of Fionn Choire. After this the path steepens and climbs up beside the burn to the lip of the corrie, where the gradient eases and the path takes a direct line across the floor of the corrie. The A'Chir ridge, to the left, is spectacular from here, but the most dramatic view is to the right, to the Rosa Pinnacle on Cir Mhor. Climb the headwall of the corrie on a beautifully pitched path, which goes up in a series of zigzags to emerge onto the ridge at its lowest point. Join the path from A'Chir to Cir Mhor at a small cairn and turn right along it.

3 This path is not made up, but is quite obvious. It climbs up above the corrie; it is somewhat eroded in places so care must be taken, but it is not difficult. It gets steeper towards the top. The final pull up the summit block is on rock but is quite straightforward although you may have to use your hands. Be prepared; the summit is tiny and the drops can be daunting. It is not a good place if you have no head for heights. The views are spectacular; you are right in the heart of the Arran hills and jagged ridges surround you on all sides.

4 The easiest way down is to retrace your outward route, first to the Fionn Choire and then down and along Glen Rosa.

Buzzard

Practicals

Type of walk: This is probably the easiest approach to this fine mountain. It is a long and fairly strenuous walk on good paths and involves some unavoidable but easy scrambling. The summit is very small and exposed.

Total distance:	11½ miles/19.5km
Time:	6–7 hours
Maps:	OS Explorer 361/Landranger 69

Walking Scotland Series
from
Clan Books

MARY WELSH has already compiled walkers' guides to each of the areas listed; material for guides covering the remaining parts of Scotland is being gathered for publication in future volumes.

Titles published so far:

1. WALKING THE ISLE OF ARRAN
2. WALKING THE ISLE OF SKYE
3. WALKING WESTER ROSS
4. WALKS IN PERTHSHIRE
5. WALKING THE WESTERN ISLES
6. WALKING ORKNEY
7. WALKING SHETLAND
8. WALKING THE ISLES OF ISLAY, JURA AND COLONSAY
9. WALKING GLENFINNAN: THE ROAD TO THE ISLES
10. WALKING THE ISLES OF MULL, IONA, COLL AND TIREE
11. WALKING DUMFRIES AND GALLOWAY
12. WALKING ARGYLL AND BUTE
13. WALKING DEESIDE, DONSIDE AND ANGUS
14. WALKING THE TROSSACHS, LOCH LOMONDSIDE AND THE CAMPSIE FELLS
15. WALKING GLENCOE, LOCHABER AND THE GREAT GLEN

Books in this series can be ordered through booksellers anywhere. In the event of difficulty write to
Clan Books, The Cross, DOUNE, FK16 6BE, Scotland.

Foxglove

Peregrine